Advanced Methods of Teaching

ADVANCED METHODS OF TEACHING

Dr. T. Pradeep Kumar

M.A., M.Ed., M.Phil., UGC-NET., PGDELT., PGDHE, PGDCA., CIT (Sri Lanka), Ph.D.,

Assistant Professor,
St.Paul's M.Ed., College,
Vijayanagar, Bengaluru, Karnataka,
India.

Himalaya Publishing House

ISO 9001:2008 CERTIFIED

First Edition : 1991
Second Revised Edition : 1996
Third Revised Edition : 2005
Reprint : 2013
Reprint : 2017

Published by : Mrs. Meena Pandey for **Himalaya Publishing House Pvt. Ltd.**, "Ramdoot", Dr. Bhalerao Marg, Girgaon, Mumbai - 400 004.
Phone: 022-23860170, 23863863; **Fax:** 022-23877178
E-mail: himpub@vsnl.com; **Website:** www.himpub.com

Branch Offices :

New Delhi : "Pooja Apartments", 4-B, Murari Lal Street, Ansari Road, Darya Ganj, New Delhi - 110 002.
Phone: 011-23270392, 23278631; Fax: 011-23256286

Nagpur : Kundanlal Chandak Industrial Estate, Ghat Road, Nagpur - 440 018. Phone: 0712-2738731, 3296733; Telefax: 0712-2721216

Bengaluru : Plot No. 91-33, 2nd Main Road Seshadripuram, Behind Nataraja Theatre, Bengaluru - 560 020.
Phone: 080-41138821; Mobile: 09379847017, 09379847005

Hyderabad : No. 3-4-184, Lingampally, Besides Raghavendra Swamy Matham, Kachiguda, Hyderabad - 500 027.
Phone: 040-27560041, 27550139

Chennai : New No. 48/2, Old No. 28/2, Ground Floor, Sarangapani Street, T. Nagar, Chennai - 600 012. Mobile: 09380460419

Pune : First Floor, "Laksha" Apartment, No. 527, Mehunpura, Shaniwar Peth (Near Prabhat Theatre), Pune - 411 030.
Phone: 020-24496323, 24496333; Mobile: 09370579333

Lucknow : House No. 731, Shekhupura Colony, Near B.D. Convent School, Aliganj, Lucknow - 226 022.
Phone: 0522-4012353; Mobile: 09307501549

Ahmedabad : 114, "SHAIL", 1st Floor, Opp. Madhu Sudan House, C.G. Road, Navrang Pura, Ahmedabad - 380 009.
Phone: 079-26560126; Mobile: 09377088847

Ernakulam : 39/176 (New No. 60/251), 1st Floor, Karikkamuri Road, Ernakulam, Kochi - 682011.
Phone: 0484-2378012, 2378016; Mobile: 09387122121

Bhubaneswar : Plot No. 214/1342/1589, Budheswari Colony, Behind Durga Mandap, Laxmisagar, Bhubaneswar - 751 006.
Phone: 0674-2575129; Mobile: 09338746007

Kolkata : 108/4, Beliaghata Main Road, Near ID Hospital, Opp. SBI Bank, Kolkata - 700 010. Phone: 033-32449649; Mobile: 07439040301

DTP by : Harshali

Printed at : M/s. Aditya Offset Process (I) Pvt. Ltd., Hyderabad. On behalf of HPH.

PREFACE

Teaching involves a set of activities called teaching acts, teacher behaviours and a number of variables that form part of the teaching process. A theory of teaching must provide a framework for the proper planning, organization and control of the teaching tasks or teacher behaviours and manipulation of all the involved variables in order to realise the stipulated educational objectives effectively, it must help the teachers to bring about desirable behavioural change, in their students and actualise their potentialities to the maximum. Teaching must provide an answer for all questions relating to teaching for effective learning. Different teaching methods like lecture method, demonstration method, inductive–deductive method, heuristic method, problem solving method, project method, etc., are used for presentation of the subject matter to the students. Any method which teacher uses is always selected and directed to serve the purpose of presenting the subject material as effectively as possible.

Models of teaching have been developed to help a teacher to improve his/her capacity to reach more children and create a richer and more attempts to create efficient systems by sequencing learning activities and shaping behaviour by manipulating reinforcement. Advanced Methods of Teaching is such a bunch of information which helps both teacher as well as students to grab the required learning activities. So all these concepts has been introduced in a simple language to enable the readers grasp them with ease. The changing perception of education is the main source of inspiration to design this book. Several other sources both print and electronic media was helpful for the writer of this book.

I express my gratitude to Publishers Niraj Pandey and Meena Pandey of Himalya Publication House, Mumbai and my heartfelt thanks to Vijay Pandey, regional manager of Bengaluru division. This book is dedicated to My Late Father, J.V. Thimme Gowda and my family members, Mother Nagarathna, Brother T. Santhosh Kumar–Software engineer, USA, Keerthi—Principal, St.Mary's Institution, Vijayanagar, Bengaluru, my teachers and mentors Dr.M.S.Talawar, Dr. H.M.Kasinath, Dr. K.B. Praveen. Dr. Jahitha Begum, Dr. G.Sheela with whose support and co-operation this work was possible.

Dr. T. PRADEEP KUMAR

CONTENTS

DETAILED CONTENTS

Chapter 1

Theories of Teaching

Objectives

After reading this Unit, you should be able to:

- Explain the teaching concept
- Explain the relationship the teaching and learning
- Understand anatomy of teaching.
- Describe phases of teaching.
- Explain the need and functions of teaching theories
- List out types of teaching theories

INTRODUCTION

Concept of Teaching

A concept is a focus of inferences permitted by the various uses of a term. Hence for understanding the concept of the terms teaching, the following issues have to be focused.

(i) Definitions of the term teaching.

(ii) Nature and characteristics of teaching.

(iii) Its relationship with other related or synonymous terms.

Definitions of Teaching

H.C. Morrison (1934): "Teaching is an intimate contact between a more mature personality and a less mature one which is designed to further the education of the latter"

John Brubacher (1939): "Teaching is an arrangement and manipulation of a situation in which there are gaps and obstructions which an individual will seek to overcome and from which he will learn in the course of doing so."

B.O. Smith (1960): "Teaching is a system of actions intended to produce learning."

N.L. Gage (1963): "Teaching is a form of interpersonal influence aimed at changing the behaviour potential of another person."

Edmund Amidon (1967): "Teaching is an interactive process, primarily involving classroom talk which takes place between teacher and pupil and occurs during certain definable activities.

B.O. Smith (1963): "Teaching is a system of actions involving an agent, an end in view, and a situation including two sets of factors those over which the agent has no control (class size, size of classroom, physical characteristics of pupils, etc.) and those that he can modify (ways of asking questions about instruction and ways of structuring information or ideas gleaned.)"

Clarke (1970): Teaching refers to "activities that are designed and performed to produce change in pupils behaviour"

Thomas F. Green (1971): "Teaching is the task of teacher which is performed for the development of a child."

Yoakum and Simson: "Teaching is the means whereby the experienced members of the group guide the immature and infant members in their adjustment of life."

Analysis of these definitions: Morrison (1934) takes teaching to a disciplined process in which a teacher by virtue of his ideal position, status, knowledge and experience influence behaviour of the less experienced pupil and helps him to develop according to the needs and ideals of the society or government. Here the student has to learn and develop according to the ideals set before him by the teachers. Teaching is reduced to what the teacher teaches. There is no interaction but there is a flow of instructions from the teacher. As a result, the pupils are bound to become passive listeners and blind imitators.

Brubacher (1939) takes teaching to that position where the pupils play the central role and teacher task is limited to arrange and create situations for the learning. Here the students have to decide what they want to do and how they will do it. This type of teaching leads the pupil to independent learning and problem solving.

Smith (1960) terms teaching as an organized system of specific activities that are aimed to help the learner to learn something. Teaching may be carried out in the absence of a teacher. Anything like a book, nature, teaching machine, etc., may play the role of a teachers. The important thing is the role of a system of actions or activities. If this system of activities result in some type of learning then this system may be termed as teaching. This definition does not consider all the 3 elements of teaching process namely, the teachers, taught and the subject matter. To overcome this weakness Smith elaborated his definition (1963) by considering teaching as a tripolar process involving:

(i) an agent (the source, human or material that tries to produce learning)

(ii) a goal or target that is to be achieved through the process of teaching and

(iii) the intervening variable consisting of learning/teaching situation or environment. It may involve physical or human material conditions and instructional methods.

Gage (1963) defines teaching as a process of establishing interpersonal relationship between the teachers and taught as a result of which the behaviour of the latter is modified. Here the relationship play the key role. But this approach to teaching-learning does not consider the role of hardware (teaching machines, programmed instruction etc).

Amidon (1967) considers teaching as a process of interaction between the teacher and the taught. He considers teaching as a co-operative enterprise, and a commonly shared phenomenon. It is two way and results in the improvement and development of both the participants, i.e., teacher and the taught. It considers teaching as a set of properly planned and clearly defined activities that are undertaken for the achievement of certain objectives. This definitions confines teaching within the interaction of the teacher and exclusively in the form of classroom talk or a few special activities.

Clarke (1970) has tried to broaden the scope of teaching by terming it as a set of all those activities that may result in bringing some change in the behaviour of the learner.

Green (1971) tried to delimit the boundary and scope of teaching task. He defines teaching as a profession or occupation by stating that teaching is what a teacher does for the development of a child. But teaching can neither be restricted to a profession or occupation of people or a community like teacher nor it can always be relied for bringing desirable improvement or development in the behaviour or function of the child. It may result in desirable as well as undesirable ways. Hence it cannot be assumed to play a developmental role in all situations.

Some of the above definitions have a very limited view of the functions and scope of teaching while others elaborate it to the extent of unbridled freedom and undefined tasks of purposeless outcomes. A single definition cannot explain the term teaching comprehensively and functionally. A good definition of teaching, clearly indicate

- Whether teaching is a process or product.
- Its constitutional elements or factors.
- Its objective
- its organizational and structural aspect.

The comprehensive and functional definition of learning may be as given below:

Teaching is a triadic relation – involving the source of teaching (human or material), student and a set activities designed and manipulated primarily to bring changes in the behaviour of the student.

Teaching is a social process. The political system, social philosophy, value and culture of a nation leave their impression on it. The meaning of teaching varies with the political system. The meaning of teaching varies from autocratic, democratic and *laissez-faire* set up.

Morrison defines teaching from autocratic point of view, Gage has democratic point of view and Brubacher takes the *laissez–faire* point of view to define teaching.

Some of these definitions consider teaching as a bi-polar process (teacher and pupil are 2 poles) and some consider teaching as a tri-polar process (teacher, pupil, and society. Curriculum is the 3 pole).

Nature and characteristics of other similarities

1. Teaching is a complex social phenomenon. It is influenced by the social factors; the social and human factors are dynamic.
2. Teaching is both an art as well as a science. Comparing to the practice of medicine, Silvermann says – it is an art as it needs talent and creativity. Like medicine it is also a science as it involves as repertoire of techniques, and skills that can be systematically studied and described and improved. A good teacher like a great doctor is one who adds creativity and inspiration to the basic repertoire.
3. Teaching is a professional activity involving the teacher and the student and which results in the development of the student.

4. Teaching is what a teacher does with his student for causing the latter to learn something.
5. Teaching is a system of actions which are varied in from and are related to content and pupil behaviour in context with the prevailing physical and social condition.
6. Teaching is highly dominated by the skill of communication. The flow of communication within the teaching elements like teacher or sources of teaching, student and the teaching activities make teaching a reality and a success.
7. Teaching may have various forms like formal and informal, formational or informational, directional or instructional, teaching conditioning or indoctrination, telling, showing or doing, descriptive or remedial etc.
8. Teaching is a specialized task and may be taken as a set of component skills for the realisation of a specified set of instructional objectives.
9. Teaching is amenable to scientific observation and analysis. What is going on in teaching, in a teacher can be observed, analysed and assessed through teaching behaviour, pupil-teacher interaction and the changes brought in the behaviour of the pupils. Such analysis and assessment may provide essential feedback for bringing desirable improvement in this process.

The relation of teaching with other similar or related concepts:

Terms like conditioning, training, instruction and indoctrination and are mistaken to be synonymous to teaching, these are various modes of teaching. Each of them contributes towards teaching. Teaching is a larger concept and each of these terms is a part or aspect of this large concept.

Teaching, as a whole, is aimed to bring changes in the behaviour of pupils. These changes may occur through

(i) teaching them how to do or perform a task or act to a situation or stimuli.

(ii) teaching them things that may enrich their knowledge and formulation of a system of beliefs.

The first type of teaching (conditioning or training) may result in shaping of behaviour and conduct. The second (instruction or indoctrination) works as a potent agent for acquisition of knowledge and formation of beliefs

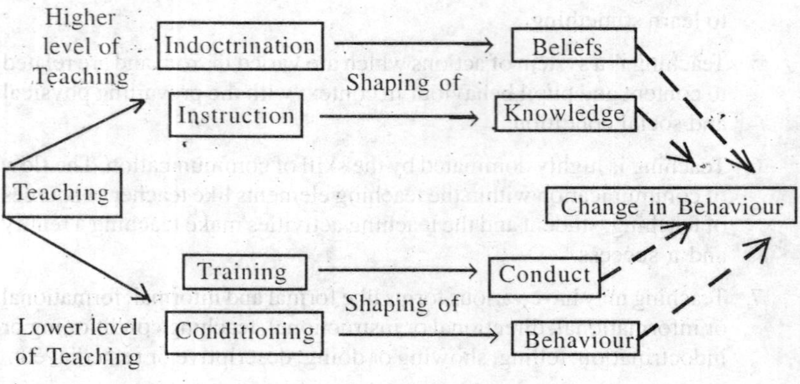

Fig: Relationship of the term teaching with other related concepts.

Teaching activities are primarily divided as high or low orders and are distributable along a continuum from conditioning to indoctrination.

Conditioning is the lowest level of mode of teaching. (Ex. Animals/ Man taught to respond to signals) It shapes our behaviours and habits. Training is the next higher level of teaching. It helps in shaping conduct and teaching various skills. (Training a particular skill of working or machine skillfully, animals – Circus tasks).

Though instruction and indoctrination are higher levels of teaching than conditioning and training, they cannot be equated to teaching, they need involvement of intellectual powers. Instruction is mainly concerned with the development of knowledge and understanding about a system, thing or process (in an individual). Imparting of knowledge and understanding is not the only objective of teaching. It is only a part of objectives of teaching. Teaching is more than the act of giving knowledge and understanding. The cognitive and affective domains of one's behaviour are neglected in instruction. While teaching is aimed towards shaping a total man, instruction cares for only development of intellect and affects the cognitive domain of one's behaviour.

The process of teaching and instruction also differ. There is a face to face interaction of the teacher and the taught in teaching but is not essential in the process of instruction. Teacher can be replaced by programmed material. Computer, radio, T.V. etc. In teaching a teacher may use these devices as aids to teaching. Hence, instruction is a part of teaching and is one of the several modes of teaching instruction itself is not teaching, but teaching includes instruction.

Indoctrination (transmission of doctrine, or system of beliefs) is on the farther end of the continuum of the modes of teaching. It represents a higher level of teaching and adds to the establishment of beliefs and ideas. It requires higher order of intelligence and results in bringing stable changes in cognitive and affective domains of one's behaviour.

Like other modes of teaching, indoctrination is one of the several modes of teaching. Indoctrination means teaching, but reverse is not true. These different modes of teaching conditioning, teaching instruction and indoctrination though are different and are distinguishable; they cannot be termed as unrelated. They may overlap in their processes and outcomes sometimes.

Relationship between Teaching and Learning

It is essential to establish the relationship between teaching and learning. The understanding of relationship between teaching and learning requires the understanding of meanings of these two.

The meaning of learning can be explained by these definitions.

Woodworth defines learning as. "The process of acquiring new knowledge and new responses."

Pavlov's view is that learning is "habit formation resulting from conditioning."

Crow and Crow consider learning as "the acquisition of habits, knowledge and attitude."

In brief, learning may be defined as a relatively permanent change in behaviour (excluding the influence of growth, maturity or lesion). The teaching process is also related to realise the same objective as may be clear from the definition of teaching given by Clarke's definition teaching, i.e., "activities that are designed and performed to produce change in student's behaviour" relates teaching process to realise the same objective. It can be concluded that teaching consists of all those activities or system of actions that are intended to produce learning.

But cause and effect relationship does not exist between teaching and learning. It is not essential for a teaching to be ended with some or other types of learning. Similarly, for learning it is not essential for a learning to be initiated or handled by some or the other type of teaching. Learning may also take place without involving the formalities of teaching process.

Whenever a teacher teaches something to his class, his teaching intends to produce learning or bringing relatively permanent changes in the behaviour of the students. But it is not guarantee that what he intends will be fully realised. It may be possible that the learning outcomes for the whole class or some particular students may be absolutely nil.

Similarly if one decides to learn something, it is not essential for a teacher or teaching formalities. It can be learnt through experience, self-study or self-learning. Teaching is an interactive process involving interaction between teachers and taught but learning may be purely one sided activity needing no interaction.

According to B.O. Smith (1961) "learning does not necessarily issue from teaching, that teaching is one thing and learning is quite another" Learning is not directly proportional to teaching or *vice-versa.* Both teaching and learning may exist and function independently.

But for good, there is a need of a good relation between teaching and learning. They can be synthesised and called teaching learning process. Both teaching and learning aims the same thing, i.e., brings changes in the behaviour of the learner. So it is necessary to bring both teaching and learning together. A good teaching must always be so designed and performed as to result in maximum learning. A teacher may also be highly benefited through a well organized system of action (teaching) for achieving his learning outcomes.

Gage (1964) considers," the process of teaching and learning must be adapted to each other so as to make whatever combination of procedures pay off best."

Teaching must make a central concern of the process of education or scheme of pedagogy, the learning, in turn, should be made a central theme and goal for every teaching.

The teaching-learning process, in the formal classroom set-up, is a joint action or co-operative task carried out by the teacher and taught. Both teaching and learning aim towards the same goal, i.e., to bring desirable changes in the behaviour of the learner. For achieving this the teaching-learning task can be performed at 3 levels, *viz.*, memory level, understanding level, and reflecting level based on least to most thoughtful behaviour or modes of action (levels of teaching-learning).

Teaching is a social phenomenon/process which can be same as a way of doing work by the teacher to lead for some specific task performance. Teaching which is being task-based may primarily be structured but during the process it may become unstructured due to different strategies.

Both the process of teaching and learning which are followed simultaneously as 2 faces of the same coin are undertaken the process hand in hand. Thus, their interrelationship can be clearly analyzed by the follow-up of following procedures like:

(1) Learning is a psychological aspect which could be achieved by the process of teaching which is a social phenomenon.

(2) Teaching leads to achieve learning.

(3) Teaching affects the personality of an individual which leads to maturity being the modification of behaviour among an individual.

(4) Teaching leads to having an intimate contact with the learners with better adjustment and thus, accounts for favourable attitudinal modification which is a learning concept.

(5) Teaching is an interaction between teacher and learner which leads to achieve the objectives which in turn affects for their modification in behaviour.

Anatomy of Teaching

Anatomy – the dictionary meaning for this term indicates that it is the science of the body learnt by dissection. Applying this to "Anatomy of teaching"— it means the analytic description of teaching. Analysis concerns with the process of breaking or separating out the elements or constituents of a substance. Therefore, a description of the analytical concept of teaching would demand the separation and naming of different elements or components of the task or process of teaching in relation to its various aspects like:

(i) .Activities undertaken in the teaching task and

(ii) Educational objectives to be achieved through these activities.

Accordingly, there are several attempts made to analyse teaching in several ways in order to understand it:

- design teaching materials and methods for realising the objectives
- perform the task of teaching effectively
- evaluate and modify it (on the basis of feedback for acquiring teaching competency and proficiency)

Some of these attempts were made by Komisar, Gage, Clarke, Brown, B.K. Pani and N.K. Janjira and Ajit Singh.

Komisar (1966) tried to analyse teaching into various specific activities like introducing, demonstrating, contrasting, explaining, pronging, justifying, explicating, defining, rating, appraising, amplifying, vindicating, interpreting, questioning, elaborating, identifying, designating, conjecturing, confirming etc.

Gage (1968): Analyzed teaching in terms of teaching skills. According to him "Teaching skills are specific instructional technique and procedures that a teacher may use in the classroom. They represent an analysis of the teaching process into relatively discrete components that can be used in different combination in the continuous flow of the teachers, performance."

Clarke (1970): Endorses the views of Komisar and Gage. He analyzed teaching in terms of some specific activities that are designed and performed to produce change in students behaviour. These activities may be of cognitive, affective or cognitive nature and belong to different levels as expressed in Bloom's Taxonomy.

Brown (1975): Analyses teaching as a many sided activity which includes a host of activities like questioning, giving information, listening etc.

B.K. Passi (1976): Concludes that teaching constitutes a number of verbal and non-verbal teaching acts, like questioning, accepting, pupil response, rewarding, smiling, nodding to pupil response, movements, gestures etc. These acts in particular combination facilitate the achievement of objectives in terms of pupil growth.

N.K. Jangira and Ajit Singh (1982) have analysed teaching as: "Teaching can be analysed in terms of teachers behaviour at least at 3 levels, *viz.*,

- Component teaching skills,
- Component teaching behaviours comprising the component skill and
- Atomized teaching behaviours.

Diagrammatically this analysis could be represented as:

TEACHING

Level 1: Teaching may be analysed into various component teaching skills:

Say S1, S2, S3 ....Sn

S1	S2	S3	S4	S5	S6	S7	S8	S9	S10	S11	Sn

Level 2: Each of the component skills may be analysed into a number of component teaching behaviours,

Say, C1, C2, C3, ...Cn

S7 (component teaching skills -7)

C1	C2	C3	C4	C5	C6	C7	C8	Cn

Level 3: Each of these component teaching behaviours may be further analysed into atomistic teaching behaviours.

Say Tb1, Tb2, Tb3, ...Tbn

C4 (Component teaching behaviour -4)

Tb1	Tb2	Tb3	Tb4	Tb5	Tbn

Fig: Analysis of Teaching (Janjira and Ajit Singh)

Here the complex task of teaching is analysed into limited but well defined components called "Teaching" or technical skills of teaching.

The Asian Institute of Teacher Educators (1972) has considered the teaching skills as specifically effective in bringing about desired changes in pupils.

Thus, teaching may be viewed as a group of skills known as teaching skills. A teaching skill is defined as a group of teaching acts or behaviours intended to bring desirable changes in the pupil's behaviour.

But this approach of analyzing teaching into some specific component teaching skills and related teaching acts or behaviours has been severely criticised. The criticism is that teaching cannot be regarded just as a sum total of certain teaching skills. Though acquisition of teaching skills is very essential for a teacher, this is not all what is needed. He needs much more and therefore teaching consists of something more than the teaching skill. It involves interaction; other factors like personality, attitude, interest, way of exercising desirable influence, etc., contribute towards effective teaching. A teacher is not a simple skilled worker who has acquired certain specific skills but one who in addition to it is able to act and take appropriate decisions and exercise necessary influence for bringing desirable change in the behaviour of his pupils.

Phases of Teaching

Teaching is a complex task. It involves many activities through which pupils, learning is assisted (The successful completion of the teaching act needs systematic planning and careful execution). For successful completion of the teaching act, these teaching activities have to proceed in sequential steps. These steps or stages are known as phases of teaching. A teaching act may be systematically analyzed into three phases.

(1) Preactive Phase of Teaching.

(2) Interactive Phase of Teaching.

(3) Post Active Phase of Teaching.

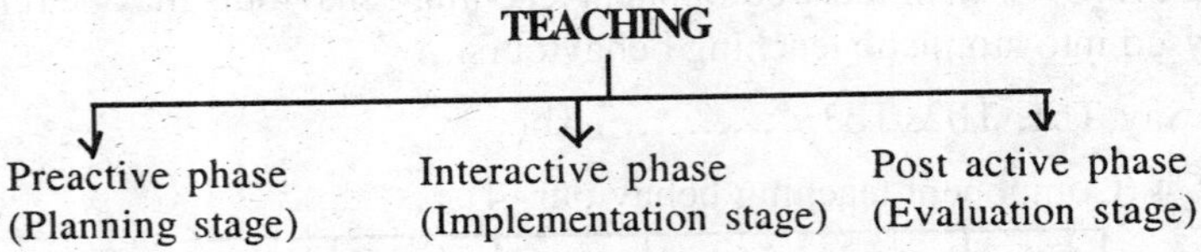

The Preactive Phase

It is the planning phase of the teaching act. A good planning makes the task of a teacher smooth, functionable and successful. The two major steps involved in this phase, namely:

(i) Establishment of goals or objectives,

(ii) Discovering ways and means to achieve these objectives.

The first step in planning for any teaching is the establishment of objectives. Accordingly the teacher has to formulate the specific instructional/teaching objectives in behavioural terms. These objectives are determined according to the psychology of the pupils and needs of the school and the society.

In the second step of the preactive phase, methods/ways to achieve the stipulated objectives are to be decided. Consequently, planning is done for taking decisions about the following aspects.

(i) Choice of the content/material to be taught.

(ii) Organization/sequencing the elements of content for presentation. (Logical/Psychological sequencing to assist maxims

(iii) Consideration about the principles and maximum of teaching.

(iv) Decisions and planning about the proper use of teaching aids.

(v) Choice of the methods, techniques and strategies of teaching

(vi) Distribution of teaching strategies (when/ how to use strategies, techniques, teaching aids, etc.)

(vii) Decisions about the evaluation tools.

In short at the preactive phase a teacher has to chalk out the details of his journey which he wants to take in the classroom along with his students.

The Interactive Phase

The second phase of teaching is concerned with the implementation of what has been planned in the previous stage. It is the stage of actual teaching. At this stage the teacher provides pupil's verbal stimulation of various kinds, makes explanations, asks questions listens to student's responses and provides guidance. The success or failure of teaching depends upon the degree and quality of classroom interaction between the teacher and pupils. The activities in this phase can be grouped as:

(a) Perception,

(b) Diagnosis and

(c) Reaction processes.

(a) Perception: Interaction process demands an appropriate perception on the part of the teacher as well as student. When a teacher enters the class, his first activity is concerned with a perception of classroom (and the size of the class). He also tries to weigh his own abilities pre-planning for teaching against the class group. Similarly the students also try to have a percept of the personality (ability/behaviours) of the teacher in order to seek desirable interaction in the teaching-learning process.

(b) Diagnosis: A proper diagnosis of the abilities and behaviour is essential for appropriate interactions. A teacher therefore, tries to assess and diagnose the achievement level of his students with reference to their abilities, academic background, intelligence, interest and attitude and aptitude. This diagnosis can be done in several ways like questioning, observing, assessing their performance/ behaviour etc. When an opportunity for performing is provided, the students can also assess and diagnose their own abilities and performance of their own response and can contribute towards effective interaction in the teaching act.

(c) Reactive Processes: Verbal interaction plays central role in CR interaction. It involves two types of activities. Initiation and Response. Both these activities occur between the teacher and the pupils. When a teacher performs some activities, the pupils react to him and when pupils perform some activities, the teacher reacts to those activities. Thus, the interaction in teaching/learning goes on. This action-reaction processes play the central role in classroom interaction. For this the teacher has to take right decisions with regard to the selection and use of proper stimuli, schedule of reinforcement (positive) and feedback devices, and (development,) deployment of suitable strategies according to the needs of the pupil, teaching environment, and teaching objectives. The pupil will react and respond accordingly to the various stimuli and teaching techniques presented to him.

The Post Active Phase

The third phase of the teaching act concerns with the evaluation activities. First of all the stipulated objectives are considered and attempts are made to assess the degree of achievement of the expected behavioural changes in the students as a result of teaching activities performed at the interactive phase. This can be done in different ways like tests, quiz, observation of student's reactions to questions, comments, structured/ unstructured situations etc. Appropriate evaluation devices are to be used by the teacher for this purpose. The result of the carried evaluation may be used by the teacher as well as students for bringing desirable improvement in their roles and activities. It may take the following shapes:

(i) The suitability of the stipulated objectives may be properly assessed. The extent or quality of their accomplishment makes them to take decisions about further continuation, alteration or improvement.

(ii) The suitability of the content and its organization may be suggested. Decision regarding teaching the content or not may, therefore be taken.

(iii) The suitability of the instructional process, aid material and teaching strategies may be evaluated. As a result strategies and techniques of teaching may be changed and improved from evidences gathered.

(iv) The classroom environment and learning situations may be evaluated. Accordingly, desired changes may be effected in management of these elements.

In the interactive phase, these activities are not only carried out by the teacher, but in order to impress themselves and to impress the students also deploy various strategies by selecting different stimuli. In this way, the interactive phase of teaching is responsible for establishing appropriate verbal and non-verbal classroom interaction between the teacher and pupils by arranging suitable teaching-learning activities and equally suitable and controlled classroom environment. Help the teacher and the students to bring changes to their performances by providing necessary corrective feedback.

Although, these three phases of teaching are described separately, they are closely interrelated. They represent a continuous cycle of teaching, influencing and directing each other as shown in the diagram.

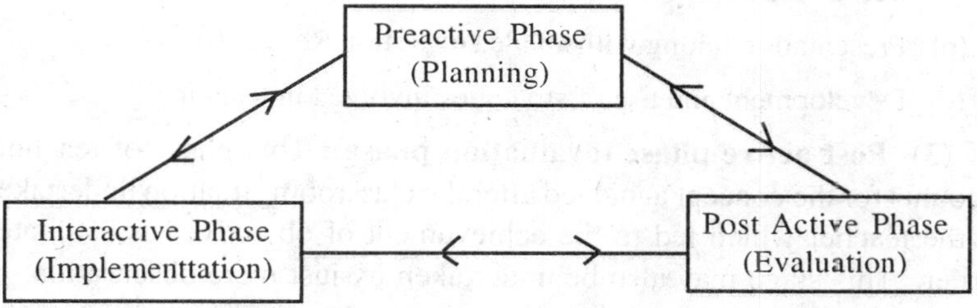

Interrelation among the phases of teaching

It can be seen that the process of teaching does not confine itself to mere classroom interaction or presentation of the contents, teaching materials or learning experiences. A teaching act cannot be confined to face to face dialogue between teacher and the students which is carried out in the interactive phase. It begins (even before the teacher can enter the classroom) with the work of planning (i.e., the teacher enters the classroom) and continues after the interactive stage in the form of evaluation, feedback and other post active activities that take place even after the teacher has left the class.

Phases of Teaching

According to Phillip H. Jackson, the operation of teaching could be classified into 3 different phases as:

(1) Pre active phase of teaching

(2) Inter active phase of teaching

(3) Post active phase of teaching

All these phases involve specific operations to be performed by,

(1) Pre active phase (planning stage): This phase accounts for a pre-estimated idea before coming to the classroom. It includes a very good estimated pre-plan of understanding the class with a "good lesson plan." Lesson plan preparation includes

- formation of objectives with a particular selected content
- content analysis
- development of strategies of teaching.

(2) Inter active phase (presentations phase): This is concerned with all activities and behaviour and manifested by the teacher in and after entering the classroom during the process of presenting the content. The operation included at this stage is:

(a) Verbal and non-verbal stimulation

(b) Presentation (along with an idea of Action Research)

(c) Development and use of strategies involved in teaching.

(3) Post active phase (evaluation phase): This phase of teaching accounts for the concept achieved after the classroom situation undertaken by the teacher which led to the achievement of objectives as estimated earlier. This stage may also be undertaken by just mere observation. It included

- testing behavioral change of students
- selection of appropriate testing device.
- feedback for evaluation

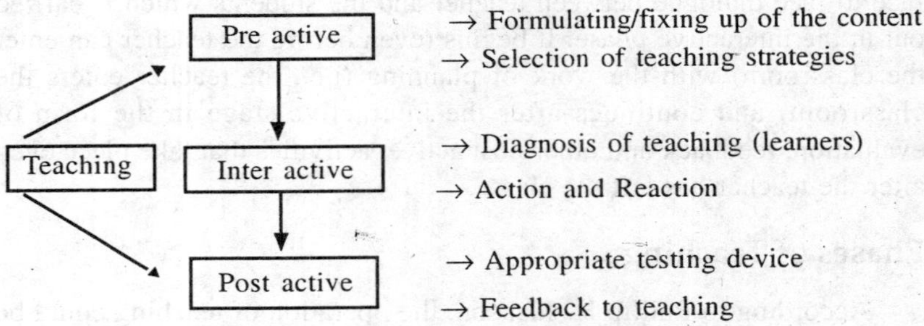

Importance of operations of teacher:

(1) To bring desirable change among the students.

(2) It is very important to perform the phases of operations in a systematic way to develop teaching skills and performance among students – teachers and regular teachers.

(3) To provide scientific basis for both teaching and learning, i.e., desired goals/objectives can be achieved to a very great extent.

A teacher should have good

- Knowledge/mastery of subject matter
- Skill of interaction with his students.
- Skill of making students learn and thinks independently
- Skill of evaluating and reinforcing pupils learning behaviour.

The psychological and epistemological bases for teaching

Teaching is a process. Teaching is not a concept but a construct. Teaching is a process of imparting knowledge. Teaching is an act which is systematically arranged and delivered so as to achieve the expected learning outcome. Teaching previously was a by polar process. Where teacher taught to interact with each other but now it is a tripolar process where both the teacher and the subject and environment will affect the learner. And the learners are the centre of the proof of the teaching process.

Teaching is both an art and a science – more a science. It is nothing but the imparting of knowledge. Teaching itself cannot be finalized and can't give the complete meaning in itself. It has its base from the different description it has a psychological, philosophical historical, sociological, political, economical base of all these it has been constructed and finalized, Teaching has a psychological base in the following ways.

Psychological bases for teaching:

Psychology taken as a base of education is called the applied psychology. The principles and techniques of psychology have to be applied to the field of education.

- Psychology helps in understanding the learner. His growth and development.
- Provided a base about learners, intelligence, personality trait, maladjustment, motivation, problems, anxiety, further by knowing their teaching can be proved.
- Provides a base of individual differences how learning takes place, theory of learning, etc., how creativity can be enhanced.
- Provides bases for classroom management, assessment of the child, capacities, desires behaviour of the child.

Epistemological bases:

Teaching is incomplete without the philosophical base. Epistemology a branch of philosophy deals with the knowledge

- Provides base about the knowledge of the universe, time, space, the five panchabuthas, air, water, sky, earth, fire.
- Knowledge to be inculcated about different concepts like religion, morality, ethos, aesthetic, art, architecture, sculpture.
- Knowledge about self-individual, his experiences, knowledge about the surroundings and how they are helpful to man.
- Knowledge about society, politics, education, economics, painting, drawing, dancing, singing, playing, etc., that applies to a class or group of objects which have certain qualities in common.

Generalisations – higher than concepts – they state some abstract relationship between two or more concept.

Concept of a Theory

The term theory has been defined by eminent scholars.

According to Kerlinger, "A theory is a set of interrelated concepts, definitions and propositions that presents a systematic view of a phenomenon by specifying relationships among variables with the purpose of explaining and predicting the phenomena."

According to Goode and Hatt, "Theory refers to the relationship between facts and ordering of them in some meaning ways"

According to Matheson, "A theory specifies the relationship between events for the purpose of explaining the occurrence of the events and predicting future events".

A theory helps in understanding the mechanism and interrelationships among the variables involved in a phenomena or process. Theories have predictive value, the result of the particular phenomena or process can be known in advance with the help of the theories.

Theory of Teaching it's Meaning

Teaching involves a set of activities called teaching acts, teacher behaviours and a number of variables that form pair of the teaching process. A theory of teaching must provide a theoretical framework for the proper planning, organisation and control of the teaching tasks or teacher behaviours and manipulation of all the involved variables in order to realise the stipulated educational objectives effectively it must help the teachers to bring about desirable behavioural change, in their students and actualise their potentialities to the maximum. A theory of teaching must provide an answer for all questions relating to teaching for effective learning.

Contrary to theories of learning which pertains to the behaviours of the teacher, the factors, conditions and situations in which they learn effectively and outcomes of learning behaviours of the teacher and their teaching aimed for better learning.

The term, "theory of teaching" has been described by some educationists.

B.O. Smith (1963) describes theories of teaching as an attempt to describe teaching variables involved in the teacher behaviour in terms of their existence and possible interrelations for predicting outcomes of teaching.

He points that a theory of teaching needs to incorporate the following three elements.

(i) It has to mention the different teaching variables involved in the teacher behaviour.

(ii) It has to describe the possible relations among these variables.

(iii) It must predict the impact of teaching.

According to Gage N.L. (1964), a theory of teaching must answer three questions related to the teaching process.

(i) How do teachers behave?

(ii) Why do they behave as they do?

(iii) What are the effects?

Gage visualises a teaching theory to have its predictive value. The learning performance of a student shows high correlation with teacher effectiveness and this effectiveness is gained through the knowledge and study of teaching theories.

According to Bruner (1966), a theory of teaching concerns with the most efficient ways and means for optimum learning. It must specify and ensure the arrangement, most effective learning experiences, learning environment and learning methods for optimum learning outcomes.

Mitra (1972), considered a theory of teaching to be derived from the theories of psychology like theories of motivation, intelligence and individual differences. In his opinion, a theory of teaching prepares the teacher to perform his teaching responsibilities as effectively as possible (A teacher has to maintain a sort of contractual relationship between himself and his students. Through his teaching, he has to materialise this contract and for this purpose he is bound to engage in the specific teaching acts like analysis of the teaching task, setting of teaching objectives, identifying the entering behaviour of the students and selecting most appropriate teaching methods and strategies for the attainment of the set of objectives.

Thus, a theory of teaching can be described as the application of knowledge of psychology for improving classroom teaching practice and the teaching skills of a teacher.

From these definitions the nature/functions of theories of teaching can be summarized in the following way.

1. Theory of teaching is directly linked with the psychology of instruction. It may draw its material from various theories of learning, motivation etc. Theories of teaching are evolved out of the logical insight into the learning process and logical analysis of the tasks.

2. Theory of teaching explains and describes the behaviour of the teacher in the classroom in order to help the students in better learning.
3. In contrast to learning theories which are psychological in nature, teaching theory is predominantly social in nature.
4. A theory of teaching is much more than a theory of learning. While a learning theory is limited to describe, explain the nature of learning, teaching theory prescribes the factors, conditions, strategies, etc., for ensuring effective learning.
5. Theory of teaching presents a systematic view of teaching by specifying relations among variables of teaching process.
6. Theory of teaching equips a teacher with proper theoretical background and training for accomplishing this task.
7. A theory of teaching points out the proper way of effective knowledge, skill or attitude of the student.
9. Theory of teaching helps in the implementation of a contractual relationship between the teacher and the taught.
10. Theory of teaching can be used to manage teaching in terms of its planning, control and prediction.
11. A theory of teaching describes, justifies, explains and suggests the most appropriate way of manipulating the elements and variables involved in the teaching process.
12. A theory of teaching which works well in a particular teaching-learning situation, may not be suitable in others. As teaching is a complex phenomenon comprising of many diversified activities, no single teaching theory can be prescribed for all the teaching-learning situations.

The aim of the process of teaching is to help the students in their learning tasks and in their development. For the realisation of this aim the teachers have to equip themselves adequately. The teaching activities are practical in nature and need a lot of theoretical support. (Bridge construction needs theoretical, pre-planning, guidance and preparations).

A teacher has to understand the nature of his job, his teaching tasks and his responsibilities towards building his students future and developing their potentialities. Hence, the need of a theory of teaching is felt on account of the following purposes served by it.

1. It helps in understanding the nature and process of teaching by describing (a) what is teaching? (b) analyses of teaching, (c) relationship between teaching and learning and (d) conditions and factors affecting teaching-learning etc.

2. It helps in the proper formulation of teaching objectives, defining these objectives in behavioural terms and explaining how these objectives can be effectively achieved by suggesting appropriate teaching techniques and strategies.
3. It helps in understanding the role of different variables involved in the teaching process, their interrelationships and manipulations in order to achieve maximum learning.
4. It helps in developing proper teaching models, teaching and instructional designs, and teaching systems for a particular teaching-learning situation.

Thus, teaching theory tries to equip the teachers with all essential knowledge, facts, principles and theoretical understanding related to their teaching tasks, behaviours and teaching process. It provides general and specific directions for the teachers in their teaching path to become effective teachers.

According to H.C. Morison (1934),

"Teaching is an intimate contact between a more mature personality and a less mature one which is designed to further the education of the latter".

According to N.L. Gage (1962),

"Teaching is a form of interpersonal influence aimed at changing the behaviour potential of another person."

Functions of theories of teaching :

(1) It helps to understand the nature of teaching.

(2) It explains the relationship and role of different variables in teaching process.

(3) It gives the knowledge about the assumptions of teaching activities which provides guidelines for organising teaching.

(4) It explains the relationship between teaching and learning and identifies a common factor.

(5) Instructional designs can be developed with the help of theories of teaching.

(6) It provides the scientific basis for planning, organizing leading and evaluating the teaching (classroom management).

(7) It helps in studying the classroom teaching problems scientifically (Action Research)

(8) It can develop teaching skills and strategies with employing competency by the use of theories of teaching.

(9) It helps for achieving the teaching objectives successfully.

(10) N.L. Gage suggests that, it may be used to increase understanding, prediction and control of teaching.

Bases of theories of teaching :

According to Freight, "Theory is a set of assumptions which would be derived by purely logic-mathematical procedures with a large set of empirical laws. It furnishes an explanation of these laws and unifies the originally relative heterogeneous areas of subject matter characterised by those empirical laws."

Teaching: The terms teaching refers to:

- Body of knowledge, a body of ideas and a system of beliefs.
- An occupation of a profession in which teacher instructs and educates.
- A way of marking something known to others usually in the routine of a school.

Bases: A combined idea of both theory and teaching leads with some important bases. Such bases of theories of teaching are:

(1) Epistemology

(2) Logic

(3) Psychology (You are already aware of the concept of psychology)

(1) Epistemology: A branch of philosophy which deals with the structure and functions of knowledge.

- It refers to the content of an education system.
- It accounts for quality and quantity of education.
- It is an quantitative measurement with a deliberate planning.

(2) Logic: It is a sequential form of thinking.

- It accounts for reasoning which is a sort of convince and mental adjustments.
- It accounts for indo-deductive approach which is the whole of sequencing.
- It is logical inductive approach thus leads to greater thinking process.

Theories of Teaching

According to Bruner (1964), "Theory of teaching is an explanation of general methodology of teaching."

According to Kerlinger (1965), "A theory of teaching is a set of interrelated constructs, definitions, propositions which presents a systematic view of teaching by specifying relations among variables with a purpose of explaining and predicting."

Types of theories of teaching

Theories of teaching are broadly classified into 3 types as

(1) Formal theories of teaching

(2) Descriptive theories of teaching

(3) Normative theories of teaching.

(1) **Formal theory of teaching:** This theory of teaching is also known as "philosophical theory of teaching," It is based on certain logic, metaphysical and epistemological assumptions and proposition. This includes:

 (a) Maeuitic theory of teaching

 (b) Communication theory of teaching

 (c) Moulding theory of teaching

 (d) Mutual enquiry theory of teaching.

(2) **Descriptive theory of teaching:** These are based on imperial evidence and observations called as descriptive theory. Its purpose is to predict the relationship between effectiveness of different variables of teaching: It includes some of the theories like:

 (a) Gagne's Hierarchical theory

 (b) Atkinson's Decisions-theoretic analysis of optimizing learning.

 (c) Bruner's Cognitive theory.

(3) **Psychology:**

 – It is based on the criteria of conditions of learning.

 – It also accounts for theories of learning.

 – It also leads to the development of personality which is a psychological concept.

FORMAL THEORIES OF TEACHING

These theories are based on certain principles of thought, science of knowledge and philosophical theories of teaching.

The following theories are formal theories;

1. Maeuitic theory of teaching
2. Communication theory of teaching
3. Moulding theory of teaching
4. The mutual inquiry theory.

1. Maeuitic theory of teaching: It is an earliest philosophical theory which originated from the ideas and methodology of teaching put forward by the ancient Greek philosophers Socrates and Plato. It also reflects the educational philosophies of Indian educationists like Vivekananda and Gandhi. There philosopher's assumption is that all knowledge rests within the individual child and the task of teaching is to unfold this knowledge. Teaching has to draw out the best in child's body, mind and spirit, and nothing has to be induced from outside. The teacher's job is to help the child in the recollection of the stored knowledge existing in the child's mind. The child has all the inherent potential (like a seed). Teaching has to provide adequate opportunities for the proper germination and growth of these potentialities. The special features of this theory are:

- The knowledge to be gained by the child through education already lies within him in the shape of forgotten knowledge. The task of teaching is to help the child in its proper recollection.
- Every child is born with inherent capacities and abilities. Teacher's job is to help the child in actualising these potentialities and making his internal, external.
- In the upbringing and education of the child, this theory puts more emphasis on hereditary than environmental influences.

2. Communication theory of teaching (Teaching Methods): Quite contrary to maeuitic theory, this theory believes that the child has nothing with him like forgotten knowledge or inherent capacities which need to be unfolded through teaching. Knowledge, skills, attitudes or interests have to be given from outside. It is not the child but the teachers who are pre-equipped with knowledge and skills; through teaching it is their duty to communicate the same by adopting proper methods to the child for his development. Variety of methods and devices like narration, explanation, demonstration, experimentation, etc., could be used by the teacher for making his communication as effective as possible. This theory considers teaching as a way of effective communication. Excellency of a teacher depends on how well the teacher is able to communicate to his students for bringing desirable changes in their behaviour.

On philosophical basis this theory is considered and conceived through the Herbartion assumption of appreciative man i.e. assimilation of new experiences to a man, already existing in the mind (consisting of past experience and old ideas). Consequently communication theory advocates that while communicating with their students, teacher (i) must make use of their past experiences. (ii) Should make use of explanation, narration and demonstration activities, as methodology (iii) should try to make maximum use of their student's memory and perceptual abilities (iv) must follow the five famous Herbartion steps–preparation, presentation, assimilation, organization and recitation while planning their lesson.

The main features of communication theory are:

- What is to be taught to the child lies outside and not within the child?
- The teacher has to provide the knowledge, skills, etc., to the child by using the communication strategies involving telling, showing and doing activities.

3. Moulding theory of teaching (Environmental play a key role): This theory considers teaching as a process of behavior modification or a way of shaping and moulding the student's behavior and personality in a desired pattern. It is the outcome of the ideas propagated by the school of behaviourism and involves the principle of stimulus response theories including operant conditioning. As a result in the teaching advocated by this theory, environmental influences hold the key and thereby whole attention is paid towards setting the proper environment for the teaching and arranging most appropriate language experiences leading to the satisfactory and rewarding results. Care should be taken to provide immediate reinforcement for the shaping of sound conduct, attitude, beliefs along with the assimilation of right knowledge and useful skills.

The essential features of this theory are:

- Environmental influences play a great role in the shaping and moulding of human behavior and personality.
- Teaching is nothing but an attempt for the proper organisation of environmental influences to help the child in the shaping and moulding of his behavior in a desirable way.

- In the process of teaching due care should be taken to maintain proper link between the stimulus and response by arranging relevant learning situations.
- The teacher's main task lies in arranging proper learning situations and provides reasonable freedom to the child for learning and developing his potential in a desired way.
- Sensation and perception play a key role in the process of communication
- For better communication, the new knowledge should always be linked with the past experiences and old knowledge possessed by the students.
- Hereditary and environmental factors, both should be provided due importance in the process of teaching.

4. The mutual enquiry theory: This theory believes that a child is very curious by nature and he is in the habit of acquiring knowledge by putting questions or making inquiry about thing and happenings. Therefore, teacher's main duty lies in arranging the learning situations in such a way as to help the child to discover the knowledge by him through enquiry. This has to be done by investigating about;

- The nature, interest and basic potential of the child,
- The nature of the subject matter or learning experiences to be acquired through enquiry
- The method of enquiry suited to the nature of the subject and needs of the learners and
- The nature of the environmental setting that can be helpful in making use of such enquiry and problem solving approach.

According to this theory, teaching becomes a cooperative enterprise in which both the learner and teacher engage in the process of enquiry and achieve the desired instructional objectives by adopting enquiry and investigating approach. Here the task of acquisition of knowledge by the learner becomes possible through a proper environmental setting in which the child is helped to achieve the desired instructional objectives with limited guidance from the teacher. He is helped in discovering the knowledge by himself instead of its mere telling by the teacher or reproduction by the teacher. The teaching- learning process is shared by the learner and teacher through mutual enquiry by raising questions, sharing the discovery of new knowledge and arriving at the new and novel ways of solving the problems.

The main features of this theory are:

- Knowledge is best acquired through enquiry and investigation.
- Better teaching involves the organisation of teaching learning situations in such a way as to help the child to discover knowledge with limited guidance from the teacher.
- Teaching and learning is a cooperative enterprise in which both teacher and learner have to participate by adopting enquiry and problem solving approach.
- Teacher and learner both should try to select most appropriate method for the enquiry and investigation depending upon the nature of the subject matter, available environmental settings and stipulated instructional objectives.
- This theory recommends the use of methods promoting mutual enquiry such as enquiry training method, heuristic or discovery method and problem solving method.

Descriptive Theories of Teaching

Theories of teaching which try to describe the variables involved in the process of teaching in terms of their interrelationships and predicated effectiveness are called descriptive theories of teaching. These descriptions are based on empirical evidences and objective observations. Since they are also predictive and prescriptive in nature they are also called Prescriptive theories of teaching. They prescribe and point out the proper way of organising instructional process for achieving the desired instructional objectives and consequently these are responsible for the origin of a number of theories of instruction like;

(1) Gagne's Hierarchical Theory of Instruction.

(2) Atkinson's Optimal Learning Theory of Instruction.

(3) Bruner's Cognitive Theory of Instruction.

Gagne's Hierarchical Theory of Instructions

Robert Gagne (1970) provided a theory of instruction based upon his own ideas about types and conditioning of learning. Main ideas of his theory of instruction are summarised below:

(1) First of all Gagne provided eight types of learning and arranged them in a hierarchical order proceeding from simple complex as:

(i) Signal learning

(ii) Stimulus response leaning

(iii) Chaining

(iv) Verbal association

(v) Discrimination learning

(vi) Concept learning

(vii) Rule learning

(viii) Problem solving

The 8 types of learning arranged in a hierarchical order clearly set the way in which a child learn by following the maxim 'simple to complex' Accordingly Gagne asserted that the teacher must place his instructional strategies so as to suit the sequential order of hierarchy of learning for leading the child from simple to complex.

(2) Later Gagne and his associate Briggs (1972) identified five learning outcomes associated with his eight types of learning, *viz.*,

(i) Motor skills

(ii) Verbal information

(iii) Intellectual skills

(iv) Attitudes and

(v) Cognitive strategies and arranged them in a hierarchical order.

Based upon this hierarchy Gagne proposed that the instructional procedure must be so planned as to suit the hierarchy of learning outcomes, i.e., the child should be made to learn the motor skills and provided with verbal information before teaching him intellectual skills and other cognitive strategies.

(3) Gagne (1977, 1979) working on the similar lines after this he proposed conditions that must be satisfied if learning is to take place. There conditions were named events/phases of learning. A child has to pass through these events in a hierarchical order while engaging in a learning task. Since instruction is meant for helping the child to learn, the events of instruction or instructional strategy should essentially be linked with the events of learning. The events of learning as proposed by Gagne in his theory of instruction have been presented ahead in a hierarchical order in the figure.

External conditions (Learning events)	Internal conditions (Process in learner's mind)	Instructional evidence
Motivation phase	Expectancy	→ (i) Activity motivation, Informing learning of The objective
Apprehending Phase	Attention: Selective Perception	→ (ii) Directing attention
Acquisition phase	Coding: Storage entry	→ (iii) Stimulating recall → (iv) Providing learning guidance
Retention Phase	Memory storage	→ (v) Enhancing retention
Recall Phase	Retrieval	
Generalisation Phase	Transfer	→ (vi) Promoting transfer of Learning
Performance Phase	Responding	→ (vii) Eliciting perform by reinforcement providing feedback.
Feedback Phase	Reinforcement	

Gagne's theory suggests to lead students through a series of instructional events that have been identified as associated with learning events and conditions essential for learning.

The above diagram illustrates that an act of learning consists of eight phases. Each of these 8 phases includes external conditions or events that are to be structured by the learner or teacher.

For example: At the motivational phase, the learner needs to be motivated. It may be done by the learner himself, or the teacher has to create events or conditions for motivating the learner.

Each external conditions or event of learning is associated or paired with the internal events or conditions, the process going on within the learner's mind. For ex., the events of motivation is associated with expectancy, the desire to expect or achieve something as an outcome of learning. These internal events associated with the external events or phase of learning counterparts are given in the rectangular boxes. While discussing the phases or events of learning in the process of learning Gagne pointed out the different instructional events in hierarchical order that do take place in a process of instruction.

Accordingly Gagne's theory of instruction planned the instructional strategy adopted by the teacher through the following steps.

- Get the students motivated to learn. It can be associated through creating student's interest in the learning task. To inform the learner about the learning outcomes or objectives attained may prove a good motivating force.
- Make the students attend to presented learning materials.
- To assimilate new learning material by stimulating recall of the previous related learning
- To provide sufficient guidance for learning and memorising the presented material
- To help the learners for the retention of newly acquired learning experiences
- To help the students to transfer or generalise the facts, principles or concepts to new situations.
- To help the students to demonstrate their achievement or performance and to provide them with immediate feedback.

Atkinson's optimal learning theory of instruction

Richard. C. Atkinson (1968) while working for the Computer Assisted Instruction (CAI) for dealing effectively with the problem of individual differences in learning came out with a theory of instruction leading the students to optimal learning. An instructional strategy, according to this theory it is composed of the following steps:

(1) The teacher first must lay out instructional objectives specified in behavioural terms.

(2) The teacher should then chalk out a model of the teaching-learning process by specifying the necessary instructional activities.

(3) A proper strategy is to be chalked out by measuring the attainment of each instructional objectives by designing suitable measurement scale.

(PMI, LCI, PI, CAI – methods were advocated for individualised instruction) ↓ ↓

Logo
Tutorial drill
Simulated teaching

steps
↓
(principles) – small steps
– self-pricing
– self-evaluation
– immediate reinform
– immediate feedback.

Bruner's Cognitive theory of Instruction

J.S. Bruner proposed this theory of instruction based on his ideas and assumptions which are as follows:

(1) Learning is not simply stimulus response (SR) conditioning or R>S> reinforcement but rather a cognitive process.

This cognitive process involves 3 simultaneous acts, *viz.*,

(a) Acquisition of new knowledge or information,

(b) Transformation of knowledge that one already possess and

(c) Checking the adequacy and pertinence of knowledge one has.

(2) Curiosity is the basic instinct possessed by every individual. Right from the period of infancy, knowledge is gained on account of the curiosity about the things, objects and events surrounding us and our attempt to involve ourselves in the knowledge getting process.

(3) Conceptualisation categorisation is the first major step in the process of learning. Human beings have a tremendous capacity to discriminate object/events in the environment, categorise or classify them in a generalised way. However, the child should be helped in the formation of right concepts from the very beginning. Bruner advocated the use of concepts attainment model devised by him for this purpose.

(4) The development of cognitive abilities in the human beings is a continuous processes. It takes place systematically in 3 developmental stages, *viz.*,

(a) Enactive mode/stage

(b) Iconic mode/stage

(c) Symbolic or representation mode/stage.

At the enactive stage the curious child gets access to some aspects of reality by resorting to motor responses thus, the first stage of learning consists of motor manipulation of the objects/events surrounding us. Hence, learning through manipulation of concrete objects or doing things should be a beginning step in any instructional strategy adapted by the teacher.

At the second iconic stage, the child is able to think about objects/ events through mental images. He is now capable of representing the reality of objects/events through a set of images or graphics (ex., representation of a room through rectangular diagram).

After reaching the symbolic representation stage the child starts using symbols in place of images. Here language and symbolism play the key role in representing the reality of objects/events. This is the highest stage where concrete reality can be represented and manipulated through pure abstraction.

(5) Knowledge is important but knowledge itself is not the role power. It is the acquaintance and mastery over the process of knowledge getting that is important for the proper development of an individual, For this purpose, a theory of instruction should take into account 3 things:

(a) Nature of individual child.
(b) Nature of knowledge to be received by the children.
(c) Nature of knowledge getting process.

(6) Children should not be made to repeat, reproduce, and present the ideas/ concepts/ principles but should be encouraged to learn on their own and discover by themselves. Hence, they should be given proper opportunities for having their own active involvement in the knowledge getting process. Thus Bruner writes "We teach a subject not to produce little living libraries on that subject, but rather to get a student to think..... for himself to consider matters as a historian does, to take part into process of knowledge getting Knowledge is a process, not a product".

For giving a practical shape to these ideas, he advocated Discovery Learning in his theory. By this approach, he wanted students to learn through their own active involvement in the process of learning, develop their independent problem solving skills, analyse and manipulate information and not simply absorb it, engage in the task of discovering and rediscovering and thus understanding by themselves.

(7) According to Bruner, teachers should follow a theory of instruction which helps them to achieve both goals of knowledge and knowledge

getting process simultaneously. Hence, he advocated 4 major aspects in the process of instruction:

(a) Predisposition to learn: The child should be made willing and able to learn what he is going to experience through the given instruction before starting to teach.

(b) Structuring the knowledge: The learning experiences to be given or contents to be taught should be effectively structured to enable the students to grasp and relate the knowledge as effectively as possible. It is difficult to teach everything about thing, to the students, hences it is necessary to make the students understand the basic structure of the knowledge related to a subject. They should be made to learn a generalised set of basic ideas/principles to be used in present and future learning situations. The term 'coding' was used for such generalisation by Bruner. For effective instruction, the teachers should try to seek the best coding system which helps in teaching the subject matter in such a way as to ensure maximum opportunities to generalise. A code built upon generalisation will thus help their students for a full group comprehension of the subject

(c) Sequencing the presented material: A teacher should properly and effectively sequence the subject matter and learning experiences. Since learning follows the sequence of enactive, iconic and symbolic representation of reality, the subject matter should be tailored and sequenced accord and also presented material should match the needs of the growing mind at their respective age levels. Thus, Bruner's theory of instruction emphasises first to convert knowledge into a specific structure within the grasp of students of various ages and then to sequence, thus structured material into a proper form well with their existing modes of representation.

(d) Providing due reinforcement: According to this theory, teachers should pay due attention to proper reinforcement in the instructional process. Intrinsic reinforcement should be emphasised (internal satisfaction, self-reward). Extrinsic reinforcements (rewards and punishments) may adversely affect the students attempt of self-learning and independent problem solving. Extrinsic motivation and reward tend to increase the chances of repetition of behavior and punishment for it is correction.

With these views, Bruner termed his theory to be descriptive/prescriptive as well as normative. Descriptive, because it tries to prescribe/describe rules and principles concerning affective ways of achieving instructional objects. Normative because it sets the norms before teachers in the form of necessary teaching-learning conditions for achieving desired teaching objectives. As he was a cognitive psychologist, he concentrated on devising ways and means of development of cognitive abilities of children by emphasising on independent problem solving and discovering learning.

The summary of his suggestions and guidelines in his theory are:

(1) Try to make best use of student's natural interest and instinct of curiosity.

(2) Encourage students to think and learn independently instead of giving them ready material, let them discover or rediscover it through their own efforts.

(3) Set the learning situations or conditions in such a way as to:
 - arouse children's curiosity and motivation.
 - minimise the risk of failure and
 - be as relevant as possible for the attainment of teaching-learning objects.

(4) Do not resort to spoon-feeding. Discourage students resorting to mechanical practice, repetition and reproduction of ideas. Their level of cognitive abilities and modes of representation of reality should be given due consideration while providing them any piece of instruction.

(5) Help students in proper identification and categorisation of objects and events in a particular and generalised way. Follow concept attainment model by Bruner for proper concept formation.

(6) Help students to learn the way of acquiring knowledge and thus get them acquainted with the knowledge getting process besides acquiring useful and relevant fund of knowledge.

(7) Arrange the learning material into a proper structure and sequence it properly for its adequate grasping and understanding by the students.

(8) Reinforce the learning behaviour of the students by concentrating on the measures of suitable intrinsic motivation or self-reward.

Normative Theories of Teaching

Like animal learning, human learning cannot take place under rigidly controlled conditions. We have normal conditions and set up for our teaching-learning activities. Therefore, there is a great need for theories which can explain, guide and control the variables involved in the process of teaching under normal classroom conditions. Normative theories serve this purpose. These theories throw light on the relationship among the teaching variables on the basis of observations carried out in normal teaching conditions. They set the norms for the teaching – learning conditions best suited for achieving the desired teaching-learning objectives. These theories are applicable for more generalized set of situations or conditions available in a normal classroom set-up. The following theories come under normative theories.

(1) Gage's Cognitive Theory of Teaching.

(2) Ryan's Theory of Teacher Behaviour.

(3) Mitra's Psychological Theory of Teaching.

(4) Clarke's General Theory of Teaching.

N.L. Gage's Theory of Teaching: is influenced by the ideas propagated by the school of cognitive psychology. Cognitive psychology does not allow the teacher to resort to simple stimulus response (S-R) mechanism or habit formation. It insists the teachers to use the principles of cognitive learning such as meaningful organisation of the perceptual field, information processing, independent problem solving etc., for utilising the cognitive abilities of the learners to the maximum.

The main views of Gage's theory are :

(1) Teaching task is mainly concerned with helping the students in proper comprehension or meaningful learning of the content material.

(2) They can have proper comprehension if this content material is organised, arranged and presented in a proper way by following the principle of cognitive learning. The programmed learning material is one such well structured and organised material.

(3) Teaching task consists of many activities that needs to be planned and organised according to the available situations and circumstances as given below.

- The type of learning to be played by teacher is like philosopher, motivation counselor, demonstrator, supervisor etc.
- The type of education objectives to be achieved.
- The type of learning in which the learner is to be engaged (motor, learning, concept learning, problem solving etc).
- The type of the stages or components of learning such as preparing the students to learn, sustaining their attention and interest, helping in proper comprehension, reinforcing their learning, evaluating their learning outcomes etc.

Ryan's Theory of Teacher Behaviour

D.G. Ryan put forward a theory of teaching based on the concept of teacher behaviour. According to it teaching is greatly influenced by the verbal and non-verbal behaviour of the teacher demonstrated by him in the classroom in order to induce learning. Therefore, the improvement in teaching and classroom instruction is dependent on the quality of the teacher behaviour demonstrated by the teacher in the classroom activities. Basic assumptions of teacher behaviour are:

- Teacher behaviour is a function of a situational factors present at the time of teaching and personal characteristics of the individual teacher.
- Teacher behaviour is observable and thus, can be measured in terms of desirable or undesirable behaviour for the purpose of good teaching.

Based on these assumptions, this theory of teacher behaviour suggests the following measures to bring improvement in the teaching process.

(1) The teaching-learning conditions must be so designed as to help the teachers in maintaining proper teacher behaviour.

(2) The teacher must pay due attention for picking up the desirable behaviour and personal characteristics helpful in good teaching and appropriate classroom interaction.

(3) Since teacher behaviour is observable and can be measured to a reliable extent, good technique of its observation and measurement like Flanders (Flander's interaction analysis), be practical for providing pre-service and in-service training to the teacher. Teachers may also adopt these techniques for their self-evaluation resulting in the improvement of their both verbal and non-verbal behaviour.

Mitra's Psychological Theory of Teaching

This theory was put forward by Sahib K, former director of NCERT. It attempts to apply the psychological principles in the field of teaching. The main ideas propagated by this theory are:

- Teaching needs to be restricted to the formalised instructional situation. However, it may take place in and outside the classroom and school.
- For teaching to take place, there must be at least two persons, one teacher and the other taught. These two persons need to be bound by contraction relationship. The teacher has a responsibility of influencing the behaviour of the taught in order to lead him from his entry behaviour to the set terminal behaviour.
- Teacher should formulate his teaching task based upon his knowledge of the psychological principles related to the psychology of individual differences, learning, intelligence, personality, aptitude and achievement. The teaching task so formulated may include the activities like:

(i) Analyzing teaching task
(ii) Identifying entry behaviour of the pupils.
(iii) Defining teaching objectives and
(iv) Selecting teaching strategies.

Clarke's General Theory of Teaching

This theory has been propagated by S.C.T. Clarke (1970). It is termed as general theory of teaching on account of its general nature outlined below:

- It consider teaching as a generalised phenomenon or process instead of specific one.
- It takes into account the teaching-learning situation in general common to all types of learning.
- The principles in this theory are generally applicable to all types of teaching carried out at different stages for attaining general teaching objectives.
- It gives due significance to all the variables, in general, involved at the different levels in the process of teaching.
- It talks about the general strategies adopted by a common teacher to deal with all types of learners in varied teaching-learning situations.

The views expressed by Clarke in his general theory of teaching can be summarized in three different heading are:

(i) Concept about Teaching
(ii) Variables of Teaching.
(iii) Levels of Teaching.

Concept about Teaching

This theory considers teaching as a general phenomenon rather than a specialised one. According to the teaching refers to activities (general in nature) that are designed and performed to produce change in student's behaviour.

Variables of Teaching

According to this theory, teaching process in general involves three types of variables.

(a) Independent variable: the teacher
(b) Dependent variable: the learner.

(c) Intervening variables: the teaching learning situations, curriculum, teaching aids, strategies and evaluation devices etc.

Levels of Teaching

This theory mentions about 3 levels in a process of teaching.

Level 1: It sets the stage for starting the act of actual teaching.

Level 2: The stage of actual and active teaching.

Level 3: The stage of appraisal and evaluation of the product and process of teaching.

Besides mentioning these levels, this theory provides rules and principles to be observed for carrying out a number of activities at different levels.

Principles to be observed at level 1: According to Clarke's theory a teacher has to keep in mind the following principles for creating necessary conditions to initiate the process of teaching.

1. Proper opportunity must be provided for communication between teacher and students and among students.
2. Develop teacher-pupils relationship in such a way that it may induce better teaching.
3. While teaching a group, care should be taken to build up a social environment helpful in better learning.
4. Teacher must ensure that students are sufficiently motivated to learn that students are active in the process of teaching learning.

Principles to be observed at level 2: The level 2 represents the stage of action and is related with actual teaching and learning. The Clarke's general theory of teaching provides the following broad guiding principles to be observed by the teacher.

Teacher must make use of appropriate teaching strategies that are common with

- the needs and characteristics of the learners.
- the learning theories.
- the specific curricular objectives.

Principles to be observed at level 3: Teaching activities at level 3 are related to reinforcement and evaluation of the activities carried out at level 2. This theory provides the following guidelines to teachers at this level.

(1) Teacher must have a proper assessment and evolution of students' progress in terms of realisation of set objectives.

(2) Based upon this assessment and evaluation, he must accordingly plan for reteaching, modifying and substituting the teaching strategies, bringing modification and alterations of the teaching objectives etc.

(3) For proper evolution the teacher must take care of the definiteness of the instructional objectives. Each of these objectives should be stated in definite behavioural terms incorporating the minimum level of performance demonstrated by the pupil at the end of teaching activity.

(4) It must be able to get proper feedback from the result of such assessment and evaluation.

Distinguishing teaching strategy from the similar terms and concepts :

The term teaching strategy is sometimes confused with other similar terms and concepts like teaching-methods, techniques, devices, and tactics etc., which are associated with teaching activities of a teacher. The distinction among these terms must be understood.

Differences between teaching method and teaching strategy:

Teaching strategy	Teaching tactics
(1) A teaching strategy is always goal directed and the goal is the realisation of the set teaching-learning objectives.	(1) Teaching tactics represent those activities and behaviour of the teacher which help in devising and implementing a suitable strategy for the realisation of the set objectives.
(2) Teaching strategy includes the activities both on the part of the learners and the teacher for creating appropriate teaching-learning environment for the realisation of the objectives.	(2) Teaching tactics are concerned only with the behaviours and activities of the teacherrespons-ible for creating suitable learning structure.
(3) Teaching objectives and task analysis are quite fundamental to a teaching strategy.	(3) Creation of an appropriate learn-ing structure is a central theme for teaching tactics.
(4) Teaching strategy is a quite comprehensive term which includes all what a teacher does in fulfilling his task of teaching, i.e., realisation of objectives. Thus	(4) Teaching tactics is quite a small and limited term in comparison to teaching strategy. It is a small segment, component or unit of

a teaching strategy includes teaching methods, teaching techniques, teaching aids material, teaching tacticsetc., for framing such a broad teaching learning structure as to help the learner in the realisation of the set objectives.	the teacher behaviour helpful to him for the realisation of his teaching objectives.

Methods and Strategies

Different teaching methods like lecture method, demonstration method, inductive-deductive method, heuristic method, problem solving method, project method etc., are used for our presentation of the subject matter to the students. Any method which we use is always selected and directed to serve our purpose of presenting the subject material as effectively as possible. Thus, any method reflects a particular mode of presentation of some specific contents of a subject. On the contrary, a strategy is selected and employed not only for the effective presentation of some specific subject material but also for the realisation of the pre-determined teaching-learning objectives. Thus strategy as a term is more comprehensive in its scope as well as structure in comparisons to a method. The distinction between them is summarised in the following table.

The distinction made between these 2 terms sometimes get narrower as both serve as the means for carrying out the task of teaching effectively. That is the reason why we have many common names included in both the categories like lecture, demonstration, problem solving, heuristic project etc. However, the line of demarcation is quite clear. All these may be refers as strategies when utilised as a means for the realisation of the well defined objectives. However, when, their field of application or role is limited only to the presentation of subject matter and they serve only as a mode for such presentation, these are referred to as methods and strategies.

We employ a number of tactics for the effective implementation of a teaching strategy in the same way as we employ appropriate teaching techniques and teaching aids for the effective implementation of a teaching method.

E. Stones and S. Morris (1972) defines teaching tactics as "Teaching tactics is goal linked influenced or influencing behaviour of the teacher, the way he behaves in the instructional situation in working towards the development of the strategy; units of teaching behaviour through which the teacher fulfils his various instructional roles with the students of his class from moment to moment; the components of teaching behaviour through which the teacher, the students and subject-matter interact".

From the analysis of this definition, the meaning and nature of tactics is as follows:

- Teaching tactics represent those behaviours or activities of a teacher which he works out and makes use for the development of a particular teaching strategy.
- Teaching tactics are fundamental or basic units of teacher behaviour helpful in creating suitable learning structure for realisation of set objectives.
- Teaching tactics help the teacher for playing various instructional roles from time to time in connection with the implementation of a teaching strategy.
- Teaching tactics may include all those activities and teaching behaviours–verbal or non-verbal which may be helpful in making a healthy triangular interaction among the teacher, taught and the subject matter.
- Teaching tactics help in the creation of appropriate learning structure for enabling the learner to achieve the determined learning objectives.

Differentiation between the terms teaching strategy and teaching tactics

Teaching strategy	Teaching tactics
(1) A teaching strategy is always goal directed and the goal is the realisation of the set teaching-learning objectives.	(1) Teaching tactics represent those activities and behaviour of the teacher which help in devising and implementing a suitable strategy for the realisation of the set objectives.
(2) Teaching strategy includes the activities both on the part of the learners and the teacher for creating appropriate teaching-learning environment for the realisation of the objectives.	(2) Teaching tactics are concerned only with the behaviours and activities of the teacher responsible for creating suitable learning structure.
(3) Teaching objectives and task analysis are quite fundamental to a teaching strategy.	(3) Creation of an appropriate learning structure is a central theme for teaching tactics.
(4) Teaching strategy is a quite comprehensive term which includes all what a teacher does in fulfilling his task of teaching, i.e., realisation of objectives. Thus a teach-	(4) Teaching tactics is quite a small and limited term in comparison to teaching strategy. It is a small segment, component or unit of the teacher behaviour helpful

ing strategy includes teaching methods, teaching techniques, teaching aids material, teaching tactics etc., for framing such a broad teaching learning structure as to help the learner in the realisation of the set objectives.	to him for the realisation of his teaching objectives.

Thus any task for its effective performance has to be dealt with theoretically and practically. A theory provides a framework, useful planning and scheme incorporating effective steps to be taken for performing a task or experiencing any activity as successfully as possible. Teaching is a task, undertaken by the teacher to produce desirable changes in the behaviour of the students. For performing this task effectively a teacher needs some pre-planning and theoretic understanding of activities that are desirable to set his behaviour in tune with the task to be performed by him. Theories of teaching, equip him with such theoretical understanding and framework.

EXERCISES

1. Briefly explain the concept of teaching.
2. Explain relationship between teaching and learning.
3. What is anatomy of teaching?
4. Explain the phases of teaching.
5. State Psychological and Epistemological bases for teaching.
6. Explain types of theories of teaching.

Chapter 2

Organisation of Teaching

Objectives

After completing this unit you will be able to:

- State the Teacher Function
- Explain teaching tactics and its types
- Explain the effective classroom management
- Explain the feedback and its types

INTRODUCTION

Teacher Function: The teacher has multifaceted roles to play:

Managing

(a) To manage learning

(b) To execute those learning means

I.K. Davies gives 4 types of responsibilities to the teacher as a manager:

(i) Planning of teaching: Here the teacher determines and defines the objectives. The teacher plans the curriculum in a sequence after analysing it. The teacher develops the instructional design and selects teaching aids for teaching. Here the teacher applies his/her imagination and creative powers.

(ii) Organisation: Teacher develops the teaching–learning conditions in order to achieve the stipulated objectives. These teaching–learning conditions are developed with the individual's differences in view.

(iii) Leading of teaching: The teacher encourages pupils, supervises their functions and provides them necessary guidance.

(iv) Controlling of teaching: The teacher evaluates all the pupils in the light of objectives. This evaluation is done through tests.

- Organisational functions
- Social functions
- Intellectual functions
- Managerial functions
- Mentoring functions
- Career functions
- Co-ordinatory functions
- Student welfare functions
- Classroom management functions
- Lesson (teaching–learning) Management functions
- Resource management functions
- Curricular and co-curricular functions
- Evaluatory functions
- Stimulatory/Motivatory functions

Activity in Teaching: According to Thomas, F.Green (1991), there are 3 different categories of activities of teaching. They are:

(1) Logical Activities of Teaching

(2) Strategical Activities of Teaching.

(3) Institutional Activities of Teaching.

(1) Logical Activities of Teaching: This particular concept selected to the primary elements like: Reasoning or Thinking.

The 8 logical acts which are included here are:-

(a) Explanation

(b) Summarization

(c) Inferring

(d) Reasoning

(e) Gathering evidences

(f) Demonstrating

(g) Defining

(h) Comparing

All these above mentioned acts account for the process of thinking within a teacher.

(2) Strategical Activities of Teaching: This concept is used to enhance the learning outcomes effectively. It includes 7 strategies like:

(a) Motivation

(b) Counseling

(c) Evaluation

(d) Planning (future strategies)

(e) Encouraging (through praising and rewarding)

(f) Disciplining

(g) Questioning

(3) Institutional Activities of Teaching: It is not related to classroom but to an institution. It includes 7 acts like:

(a) Collection of (money) funds
(b) Supervision
(c) Attending meetings
(d) Keeping track on attendance records.
(e) Teacher-parent consultation
(f) Maintenance of report and cumulative record
(g) Counseling

Classroom Management

It would be worthwhile to understand the meaning of the term 'management' before knowing about classroom management. It is an important function for any organization and it concerns the co-ordination and cooperation necessary for goal attainment. In simple words, 'management' stands for attempts of managing available resources (human and material)., so as to yield best possible result. The process of mobilisation and utilisation of the available men-material resources for achieving the desired specific objectives in an efficient and effective way is termed as management. In the language of system approach, it is the process of making best use of the input and transformation process to result in the best output. Management as a process involves the task of managing various important aspects like planning, organising, leading and controlling of the activities and roles of the available men-material resources for achieving the desired objectives in a best possible way.

Effective Classroom Management

Effective classroom management cannot be given as a coolbook recipe. However, research in classroom has established clearly that approaches to classroom management are more effective than others in particular that the key to successful classroom management is preventing problems before they occur.

(1) Problem prevention: The key to prevent discipline problems from occurring in the class is excellent planning and an understanding of group dynamics. In addition to this mastering of teaching skills help in preventing management problems since this gives confidence in the teacher's ability. Their task-oriented manner of behaviour tends to discourage most classroom management problems. Jacob Kounen conducted extensive research and found that the teachers who managed their classrooms successfully had certain teaching behaviours:

(a) They established and discussed clear comprehensive rules for behaviour in their first class itself.

(b) They displayed their alertness as in the proverb "eyes in the back of their head" 'wittiness' was the term used for this quality by Kounin.

(c) They used individual students and incidents as models to communicate their conduct expectations- Kounin's ripple effect.

(d) They supervised several situations simultaneously.

(e) They adjusted discipline approaches to particular students and situations.

(2) Problem solving: If management problems occur in the classroom, problem solving are to be exhibited by the teacher. Two of the most widely used structured approaches to classroom management are (i) LEAST approach (ii) Behaviour modification approach

(i) The LEAST Approach: This approach is useful especially for secondary school teachers. It is a sequence of discipline steps outlined in the LEAST program, which is found in A Design for Discipline: The LEAST Approach.

The steps are spelt out in the acronym itself.

- **Leave it alone:** Decide first of all if the misbehavior is worth noticing. Often it is not.
- **End the action indirectly:** Have the student assist (you) teacher or his fellow students with an activity. Direct the student towards an alternative, correct behaviour without a confrontation over the misbehavior.
- **Attend more fully:** This concentrates on the counseling component. The teacher needs to get to know the student better before deciding the action to be taken.
- **Spell out direction:** The teacher should specify the problem and should tell the students what is expected of them. Negative usage should be avoided and what is to be done by them should be spelt out. The consequences of neglecting the directions may have to be specified some times.
- **Track the behaviour:** The actions of the students needs to be recorded and follow up of the consequences should be made.

Teaching is a complicated job. It is much more than mere imparting knowledge to the pupils. Apart from preparing assignments, putting questions, explaining and clarifying complexities of the subject matter, the teacher is to study his pupils, their natural and acquired tendencies, needs, interests, potentialities, past-experiences etc. Teaching being synonymous with causing the pupils to learn. The successful teaching will depend on how effectively and how efficiently all the elements in the teaching-learning process are organised and managed. So, classroom management should be good.

Classroom management is the art of organising all the pupil-teacher activities," so that effective learning may take place without the least wastage of time and energy. It eliminates confusion and establishes favourable working conditions conducive to learning. Though effective classroom management comes through experience, yet a new entrant in this profession needs to be made fully conversant with all aspects of classroom management may be listed below.

(a) Regulating physical conditions of the classroom: Effective classroom work can take place only in a congenial classroom atmosphere. The classroom should be neat and clean, spacious, attractive and free from any inconvenience to the pupils work. Outside interference should also be reduced to the minimum. In the absence of the comfortable working conditions of the classroom the pupils do not feel like working wholeheartedly.

(b) Observing Routine: In order to prevent confusion and wastage of time and effort, the routine should be observed in the management of certain classroom activities such as taking roll call, entering or leaving the class room, arranging seats or other instructional materials in order, working according to the time schedule etc. Changes in such routine matters will simply confuse the pupils and necessitate new directions for every change. Routine should be followed in so far as it economises time and effort and facilitates smooth working of the class, but it should In no case mechanise the learning activities of the pupils.

(c) Using Instructional Materials Properly: The classwroom should be well furnished and equipped with the requisite instructional material and equipment. The material to be used in the period should be collected and placed at a convenient place before the beginning of the period. Nothing superfluous should be kept in the room. Ill-equipped class-room or ineffective handling of instructional materials will lead to the sheer wastage of time and may also create some disciplinary problems on the other hand; the teaching materials well planned and properly used will surely make teaching effective.

(d) Conducting Classroom Activities: Activities to be performed in the class must be purposeful and these should be planned before- hand and regulated properly. The whole procedure of work should be made clear to the pupils and the work should start promptly at the beginning of the period, otherwise the pupil develops the habit of wasting time and starting work late.

In order to save time and avoid confusion in the same or similar type of activities, certain routine, may be observed but not to the extent of curbing of pupils initiative and originality. The teacher should see that each pupil attends to his work properly and nobody shirks work.

(e) Tackling Behaviour Problems of the pupils: Apart from teaching, the teacher has to tackle numerous behaviour problems in the class. He is to deal with pupils of different abilities, interest, taste and socio-economic background. Some pupils may create such disciplinary problems as random talking, whistling, hooting, clapping, throwing chalk, bullying, developing unhealthy competition, using discourteous language etc. The teacher should not be upset if confronted with such a problem. He should regard it as a challenge to his teaching skill. Such problems may have much to do with the teacher's personality, preparation, method of teaching, attitude towards pupils or his failure to understand the particular difficulties or needs of the pupils. He should diagnose the causes underlying the overt behaviour and apply the remedial measure accordingly. He should be kind but firm in dealing with the disciplinary problems of the pupils. He should be neither too lenient nor too harsh towards his pupils.

The teacher should come fully prepared and create congenial classroom atmosphere, so that no undesirable incident occurs in the class.

(f) Developing Social Qualities: The classroom management cannot be effective if there prevails feeling of enmity, jealousy, rivalry among different sections in the class. Mutual co-operation and goodwill are essential for smooth working of the class. The teacher should try to develop in the pupils, social qualities such as friendliness, co-operation, fellow feeling, tolerance etc. Let them work in team spirit, Each pupil should be assigned some classroom duty so that he develops a sense of responsibility and gets the chance to display his worth.

So, to manage all these activities of the classroom the teacher should be skillful and he should have favourable attitudes towards his profession. The teacher's personality should include certain necessary gifts for his work. His speech and manners should be commendable, for they will be imitated by his pupils. He should also have a sense of humor as many problematic situations can be saved by just a smile or a humorous remark instead of taking things too seriously.

Classroom Facilities

Before exactly considering the classroom facilities, let us glance over some of the facilities regarding school, like site of the school and the school building. Sufficient attention should be given to the school building. At present much attention is not paid to the school building and a school is opened wherever some space is available, and they will not consider the facilities at all, this is a bad effect on our children. We should keep many facilities in mind when raising a school building.

At the time of planning a school building, first of all one should pay attention to the place where it is to be built.

(a) Site: The school should be neither very far nor very near a city. It should be situated in a healthy environment. There should be proper arrangement for playgrounds and gardens. If in its vicinity, arrangement for a hostel and residential quarters for the teachers are made, it will be better. The place of the schools should be so spacious that an extension in the building may be possible if needed.

(b) Building: The building of the school should be impressive. Buildings which resemble the English letter T, E, L, H and U of the alphabet look very beautiful. The 'E type' of building is regarded as the best. There should be a good arrangement of windows and ventilators. The building which is single storyed is best. There should be separate rooms for teaching of various subjects.

Now let us consider the classroom facilities effective classroom work can take place only in a congenial classroom atmosphere, which includes proper adjustment of light, ventilation, temperature, seats, furniture, black-board or other instructional materials etc. The classroom should be neat and clean, spacious, attractive and free from any inconvenience to the pupil's work. Outside interference should also be reduced to the minimum. In the absence of the comfortable and necessary facilities of the classroom the pupil does not feel like working wholeheartedly.

Let us know in detail about each facility which is needed for a classroom, the size of the class-room should be in proportion to the number of students and the area occupied by the school building. If the number of students is big, a larger classroom will be required. There should be good provision for light and ventilation in classroom.

(c) Blackboard: Blackboard is considered as second tongue of the teacher, a good board will also be needed for a classroom. Two kinds of blackboard are used in our schools: (a) The wall-studded and (b) Wooden blackboards. From the point of view of teaching the wooden black boards are more useful. These can be used even when classes are taken outside the classroom. These can also be adjusted according to the light and both the sides can be utilised. It can of course be used in art classes but in other classes its use is not convenient.

(d) Desks and Chairs: In a classroom various types of furniture is also required In a classroom for each student there should be one chair and a desk so that he may do his work freely. The chairs and desks should be so arranged in the classroom that the teacher may be able to go to any student easily. The size of the chairs and desks should be according to the respective age of the student. The table of the teacher should be placed high so that he may be able to look at all the students.

We shall describe below the size and shape of the above mentioned chairs and desks in a class-room:

1. All the desks, chairs, benches, in the class-room should not be of one size. They should be of different sizes and shapes according to the age and height of the students. For small children there should be small tables and chairs and for older children bigger ones.
2. The benches should have a back rest. This makes sitting convenient and the students do not feel tired quickly.
3. The benches should be placed at right angles to the wall so that sufficient light may fall on the table.
4. The desks should provide 18 inches of space for each student and there should be space in-between the rows so that there may be no difficulty in movement in the class.
5. The surface of the table should curve inwards at an angle of 150 degree.

(e) Cupboards: In every classroom there should be many wall-cupboards which are useful and do not occupy much place. To store maps, globe etc., open shelves will be all right. To hang maps and charts and other useful articles, a string fixed to nails at 7 ½ feet or 2 metres height may be used. In science rooms there should be a number of cupboards.

(f) Teaching aids: A well or best classroom should be facilitated by all type of teaching-aids that are needed for effective teaching, like charts, blackboard, projector, maps, globe, projection-screen etc. In the classroom facts about the famous writer, poets, scientists and others should be displayed. The best extracts should be copied out and displayed. Photographs of famous national leaders, scientific literary figures should be displayed.

(g) Class Library: There should be a central library in the school, but besides this, if there are class-libraries it will be easier for the students to get books from these. The classteacher is familiar with all the students in the class and he can guide the students about the books suitable for them. In the class-library books should be selected according to the abilities and interests of the students of the class. Class-libraries enable the students to get books easily and to avoid a waste of time. Besides, the teacher by telling about different books, help to develop in the students varied interests.

Class libraries will prove very useful for lower classes, because at this stage the students are not an age to have a complete knowledge of different subjects nor do they have any interest in this. Besides in lower classes only the class teachers can tell the students which books on different subjects are suitable for them. In the class library the students should be given the facility of choosing the books for themselves.

If we provide all the facilities according to the above mentioned principles, our students will be healthy (both physical health and mental health) amenable to discipline and true servants of society.

Feedback

Feedback is an essential element in the analysis and operation of any system. Feedback should be provided at various stages.

Blind pursuit of a process without determining its effectiveness at various stages, is wasteful so, there is a need of feedback.

Definition:

According to Berlo "If communication sources decode the message that he encodes, if the message is put back to the system, he had feedback."

In other words, action and reaction interdependent in communication is referred as feedback.

According to Sherann "a constant communication of the teacher and students results as feedback."

Feedback is essential for both the teacher and also student.

By feedback the teacher can check his own effectiveness and guide to his own future actions.

In a classroom the teacher may get positive feedback or he may get negative feedback. Positive feedback are referred as regarding feedback and negative feedback are referred as non-regarding feedback. When the teacher gets regarding feedback he continues the same type of teaching. He thinks that his method is effective. If he gets non-regarding feedback he goes for a change in his methods of teaching. So, feedback is needed for teacher.

The same analogy holds good in case of learner also if the learner gets regarding feedback, it gives him a kind of motivation for his further work. For example, by winning prize in any competition gives him motivation, this sense of victory keeps him to perform better and better. If the learner gets non-regarding feedback he will go for a change and try to improve his activity. So feedback is needed for the learner also.

Types of feedback

There are two types of feedback. Namely (1) Intrinsic feedback (2) Extrinsic feedback

(1) Intrinsic feedback: Feedback obtained through his(student) own action is called intrinsic feedback. For example: If a student working certain mathematical problem, if he gets correct solution, it gives him a kind of self-motivation, it is intrinsic feedback. In higher-level of education intrinsic feedback plays a vital role.

(2) Extrinsic feedback: Feedback obtained from others particularly from the teachers and parents are called extrinsic feedback. In extrinsic feedback teacher guides the students to move in the right direction.

For example: The pleasant look of the parents, the praising words of the teacher are examples for extrinsic feedback.

Importance of feedback in education

(1) Feedback serves to control and correct the signal and go forward.

(2) Feedback is very important for to and fro communication.

(3) It also serves to realign. Realign means to re-arrange the system.

In the teaching-learning process if the teacher goes for a change in his methods or strategies, it brings change in the system. So feedback will bring changes in the whole system.

Teaching Tactics

In managing teaching-learning tactics the teacher creates learning conditions that help him in achieving the teaching objectives, in bringing about the expected changes in the behaviour of the pupils. These learning conditions are created on the basis of the learning objectives and the learning structures. In order to create these learning conditions, the teacher should take care of appropriate teaching tactics, teaching aids, communication methods, etc.

I. K. Davies has suggested four activities to be performed by a teacher while organising teaching.

(1) Selecting an appropriate teaching tactic

(2) Selecting an appropriate audio-visual aids

(3) Selecting appropriate class size

(4) Selecting appropriate communication strategies

Teaching Tactics are the ways of implementing teaching strategy. Different types of tactics are used in the same teaching. The tactics are more concerned with creating appropriate learning structure.

E. Stones and S. Morris (1972) have defined the term teaching tactics in the following way: "Teaching Tactics is good linked/influencing behavior of the teacher the way he behaves in the instructional situation in working towards the development of the strategy; units of teacher behaviour through which the teacher fulfils his various instructional roles with the students of his class from moment to moment; the component of teacher behaviour through which the teacher, the students and subject-matter interact."

A tactic of teaching is a unit of teacher behavior which is helpful for achieving instructional objectives. A tactics may range from non-verbal behaviour to more complexes verbal behaviours of a teacher behaviour are purposeful or goal linked influence.

In preparing an instruction, attempt is made to establish relationship among tactics, strategies teacher behaviour objectives of education and the learner. The instructional behaviour consists of a chain of three links-observing, diagnosing and acting functions of teaching.

Selecting appropriate teaching tactics

Teaching tactics are used by the teacher to make the teaching/content easy, precise and understandable. Teaching tactics help in making the knowledge stable. For the qualitative progress of teaching, teacher uses various tactics according to the conditions of learning structures.

As we know, each element of a subject matter has its own structure. The teacher selects teaching strategies, tactics and aids on the basis of the structure of each element of the subject matter. The learning structure associated with a particular content (element of subject matter) should be kept in mind while selecting the teaching tactic. Hence, the knowledge of learning structure is essential in order to select the appropriate teaching tactics.

The different tactics to be used in the different learning structures are:

(1) Signal Learning Structure and Teaching Tactics

Signal learning structure occurs in terms of stimulus response. The basis of this type of learning structure is stimulus response. In this type of learning structure the pupils continuously practice a response to a particular stimulus. Here the duty of the teacher is to compel the pupils to respond to the stimulus at first. Later the teacher has to overlook the wrong answers and motivate them to give correct answers. At the end, they should gradually exercise the response through reinforcement. Hence, in signal learning structure the teaching tactics to be used are:

(a) Establishing contiguity

(b) Constant practice and rehearsal

(c) Reinforcing the correct response

(2) Chain Learning Structure and Teaching Tactics

Chain learning is the establishment of sequence of facts and symbols learnt before (poetic-recitation) verbal activates and motor activities (cycling) are the basis for forming a chain.

This chain is of three types:

(i) *Progressive chain:* Starts from signals and reach up to the end.

(ii) *Rote learning:* Chain acquired through cramming

(iii) *Retrogressive chain:* Start from the last activity and reach the beginning of the chain.

The retrogressive chain is more effective, it functions as reinforcement and helps in acquiring efficiency in the task. Hence, the teaching tactics to be used in chain learning structure is

(a) progressive chaining

(b) role learning

(c) retrogressive chaining.

(3) Multi (Discrimination) Learning Structure and Teaching Tactics

Multi–discrimination learning structure includes both signals and chains. In this type of learning, facts are differentiated and discriminated from each other and comparisons are clearly made. For this to happen the students should be clear of two elements, i.e.,

(i) Stimulus and response should be clear and

(ii) All the concepts, facts, etc., should be presented simultaneously.

Hence in this type of learning structure the teacher should use the following teaching tactics:

(i) Distinctive Conditions

(ii) Simultaneous Presentation.

(4) Concept Learning Structure and Teaching Tactics

In concept learning structure, the students have to build up the capacity to generalise groups of actions which look different externally. These groups may be different from each other but possess some similar attributes which may be identified to name the basic concept. (For Ex: Each orange may vary in shape but all the fruits are juicy) The students may understand and identify the concept by trial and error method. But they must go through the signal and chain structures. It is only after this, they would be able to generalise. In this type of learning structure, the teacher should present various stimuli which are relevant to the concept so that all the students may generalise ideas, about that concept. Hence, he should create situations which help students in differentiating two confusing concepts (orange, lemon, and mousumbis). Thus in concept learning structure, the teacher should use the following two tactics:

(i) Generalisation within the group (class concepts)

(ii) Discrimination between groups (classes, concepts)

(5) Principle Learning Structure and Teaching Tactics

In principle learning structure, a chain of two or more concepts is included. The concepts included in the principle are related and form a chain.

For Ex: Principle: Solids objects expand in heat

This principle has 3 concepts (i) object or matter (ii) heat (iii) expand.

These three concepts are placed in one chain which form the principle and the relationship between these concepts are indicated through the statement of the principle. Hence, in order to provide knowledge of the principle learning structure, the teacher should let the students to recall the concepts and make a chain of these concepts. Hence the two tactics to be used by the teacher in principle learning structure is:

(i) Recalling the concept

(ii) Chaining the concept

Learning Structures and Learning Objectives

The learning structures and learning objectives are directly related to each other. Different learning structures have different and definite teaching tactics. Thus, by using different teaching tactics in various learning structures, various learning objectives could be achieved.

For Ex: By using tactics of signal learning structure → Knowledge objectives could be achieved

By using tactics of chain learning structure → Comprehension objectives could be achieved

By using tactics of multi-discrimination structure → Application objectives could be achieved.

By using tactics of concept and principle structure →Creativity objectives could be achieved.

Learning structures is made more precise by task analysis. Therefore, the teacher should keep task analysis, learning structures and learning objectives in mind while selecting the teaching tactics. The teaching tactics should be selected in accordance with the type of learning structure so that the teaching-learning objectives are achieved.

EXERCISES

1. State the teacher function.
2. Briefly explain teaching tactics and its types.
3. Explain the effective classroom management.
4. Explain the feedback and its types.

Chapter 3

Interaction Teaching

Objectives

After completing this unit you will be able to:

- Explain Interaction Teaching
- Briefly Explain the Flanders System of Interaction Analysis
- State the Advantages of Flanders Interaction Analysis?

INTRODUCTION

Interaction Teaching

A teacher interacts with students in a classroom using instructional materials so that the students can learn selected educational outcomes consisting of knowledge, attitudes, and skills. Interaction is the continuous stream of behaviour which occurs in the classroom as a series of individual acts. An act might consist of a teacher contacting the class or a single student. A student contacting another student or a student acting upon an object in order to reformulate knowledge. Classroom interaction refers to the chain of events which occur one after the other, each occupying a small segment of time. Teaching may be conceived as a series of overt acts over a period of time. How many different kinds of acts to be seen depends upon what one is looking for. With so much to keep track of, observers reliability would be very low and data would be too complex to analyse. Somewhere between too many and too few categories is an optimum number of categories that will permit the observer to reach psychologically useful inferences by recording acts of influence as rapidly as they can be identified.

"Interaction Analysis" in the classroom is a method of observation which can be used to quantify the qualitative aspects of verbal communication. The entire process becomes a measure of teacher's influence because it makes the assumption that most non-verbal influence is truly related with the verbal.

Interaction analysis is a specialised research procedure that provides information about only a few of the many aspects of teaching. It is an analysis of spontaneous communication between individuals, and it is of no value of which no one is talking, if one person talks continuously, if one person reads from a book or report, of the total complex is called "teaching" interaction analysis. It applies only to the content-free characteristics of verbal communication.

Interaction analysis is a label that refers to any technique for studying the chain of classroom events in such a fashion that each event is taken into consideration. An observer or students in the classroom, views a videos-sound playback, or just listens to a voice recording and keeps a record of the flow of events on an observation form. He might punch the keys of some mechanical device if it is available. He is trained to use a set of categories. He decides which category best represents each event and then writes down the code symbol of that category. His speed of recording depends on the category system, the skill of the observer, and the difficulty of the interaction, but an average speed of 10 to 30 symbols per minute can be expected. The product of his observation is a long list of code symbols, one symbol to one event. An analysis can be made of the frequency of events in each category, a profile of the distribution can be drawn or a simple display can be created which shows how each event is a part of the chain. Inferences about the chain of events can be made, keeping in mind the limitations of the overall process.

The techniques of interaction analysis capture selected elements of classroom verbal communication which proves to be helpful in the analysis of teaching behaviours first, for the improvement of instruction, second, for the preparation of future teachers, and third, for the predication of educational outcomes.

Teaching behaviour has been defined as acts by the teacher which occurs in the context of classroom interaction. An event is defined as the shortest possible act that a trained observer can identify and record. Often, during classroom interaction, the same sequence of events occurs again and again, such a sequence can be called a pattern. A pattern is a short chain of events that can be identified, occurs frequently enough to be of interest, and can be given a label (name) since this often facilitates thinking.

Even these few concepts like teaching behaviour, event, pattern etc., provide us with the tools for thinking about a number of significant questions. Can teaching be improved by identifying and practising behaviour pattern? Are there certain patterns which can be associated with more positive pupil attitudes? More extensive content achievement? More independent and self-directed pupil behaviour? Can pattern be used to describe models of teaching behaviour?

As a result of the various researches, more than hundred systems are available at present for the analysis of teacher behaviour and classroom interactions.

Richard L. Ober, *et. al.*, (1971) have tried to classify these systems into two groups:

(1) Sign systems (2) Category systems.

(1) Sign Systems: Sign systems are composed of a list of behaviours. In such system, the observer simply checks or marks in some way, each behaviour, that occurs during a given period of time. Regardless of the frequency of its occurrence the behaviour is marked only once during the observation period.

(2) Category systems: In category system, teacher behaviour is first divided into various units. A behaviour unit is then classified into categories. The discrete set of all such categories then constitutes a system known as category system, in this system, at regular intervals of the observation period (e.g., Within each 3 sec of duration), the task of an observer, consists of determining in what category the observed behaviour falls. He also takes note of the category number. Here behaviour may be encoded as many times it occurs contrary to sign system where it is recorded only once. The sequence of occurrence of various behaviours is also recorded in this system. The Flander's System of Interaction Analysis is a good example of category system.

Flanders

Flander's System of Interaction Analysis (1959)

This system of interaction analysis was developed by Ned A. Flanders in the year 1959, at University of Minnesota, in the form of a teachers training technique. It is a category type system involving categorisation of all the sets of possible verbal behaviour in the classroom while interacting with his students.

Teaching is more than talking. But the predominant instructional behaviour of the teacher is talk. Almost 70% of classroom instructional time is spent in talk either by the teacher or by students.

When a teacher talks, he may present information, praise or criticize students, give directions, ask questions or accept and help clarify student ideas and feeling. When students talk they may respond with specific information to narrow questions or initiate ideas or questions of their own. This classification of teacher and student talk constitutes the categories for the system of interaction analysis.

In the Flanders, system of interaction analysis, all teacher statements are classified first as either indirect or direct. The classification gives attention to the amount of freedom the teacher grants to the student. He can be direct, i.e., minimising the freedom of the student to respond.

In order to make total behaviour/interaction in the classroom meaningful, the Flanders, system provides for the categorising of student talk. A third major section, that of silence or confusion, is included in order to account for the time spent in behaviour other than that which can be classified as either teacher or student talk. Hence, all statements that occur in the classroom are categorised in one of the 3 major sections.

(1) Teacher talk (2) Student talk (3) Silence or confusion.

(Assumption: Verbal behaviour of an individual is an adequate sample of the total behaviour.)

The larger sections of teacher and student verbal behavior are subdivided in order to make the total pattern of teacher pupil interaction more meaningful. The two subdivisions for teacher verbal behaviour, indirect and direct teacher talk are further subdivided into smaller categories.

Indirect influence consists of 4 observation categories:

(1) Accepting feeling (2) Praising or encouraging (3) Accepting ideas and (4) Asking questions.

Direct influence is divided into three categories:

(5) Lecturing (6) Giving directions and (7) Criticising or justifying authority.

Student talk is divided into two categories:

(8) Responding to teacher and (9) Initiating talk, when it is difficult to determine who is talking the 10th category is used (10) Silence/ Confusion.

All categories are mutually exclusive, yet totally inclusive of all verbal interaction occurring in the classroom. Whenever the teacher is talking, the statements must be categorised in one of the first seven categories. If the observer decides that with a given statement the teacher is restricting the freedom of children the statement is tallied in categories 5, 6 or 7, if the teacher is responding freedom of children, the category used is either 1, 2,3, or 4.

Every three seconds the observer writers the category number of the interactions, he has just observed. He records these numbers in sequence in a column. He may also write down marginal notes from time to time, which can be used to explain what has been happening in the classroom.

The observer stops classifying whenever classroom activity is changed (for ex., when various groups are working around the classroom, or when children are working on workbooks or doing silent reading. He usually draws a line under the recorded numbers and makes a note of the new activity and resume categorising when the total class discussion continues.

Ground Rules: Because of the complexity of the problems involved in categorisation, several ground rules have been established. These rules aid in developing consistency in trying to categorise teaching behaviour.

Rule 1: When not certain in which of two or more categories a statement belongs, choose the category that is numerically farthest from category 5 (ex. out of 2 or 3 choose 2, of 5 & 7 choose 7 etc.,)

Rule 2: If the primary tone of the teacher's behaviour has been consistently direct or consistently indirect, do not shift into the oppcsite classification unless a clear indication is given by the teacher.

Rule 3: The observer must not be overly concerned with his own biases or with the teacher's intent. (ex., Sarcastic praises ! category 7 not 2) The effect of a statement on the pupils is crucial in categorising a statement and not the teacher's interest.

Rule 4: If more than one category occurs during the 3-2nd interval, then all categories used in that interval are recorded, therefore record each change in category. If no change occurs in 3 seconds. repeat that category number. {(ex., Question-child answer - praises) within 3 seconds}.

Rule 5: If silence is longer than 3 seconds, it is recorded as 10. and if two or more people talk together and there is confusion record 10.

Recording Data in a Matrix

There is a method of recording the sequence of events in the classroom in such a way that certain facts become rapidly apparent. This method consists of entering the sequence of numbers into 10 rows by 10 column table, which is called a matrix.

Ex: Observer has classified the following sequence of numbers, Sample Interaction Matrix

10
1st Pair
2nd 6
10 3rd
7 4th
6
1
1
4
9
9
9
2
3
3

First

1	2	3	4	5	6	7	8	9	10	Total	1
1			1							2	
2			1								1
3			1							1	2
4								1			1
5											0
6	1									1	2
7						1					1
8		1						11			3
9											0
10					1	1					2
Total	2	1	2	1	1	2	0	3	0	2	14

Second

Tabulation is now made in the matrix to represent pairs of numbers.The numbers are marked off in pairs. The first pair, 10-6; the second 6-10, etc., 10-6 is shown by a tally in the cell formed by row 10 and column 6. The second in cell of row 6 and column 10. Each pair of numbers overlaps with the previous pair and each number except the first and last is used twice. So a 10 is entered as 1st number and last in the record. This number is chosen as it is convenient to assume that each record began and ended with silence. It also permits the total of each column to equal the total of corresponding row. (Note: For checking the tabulation: One less tally in the matrix than the numbers entered in original record N-1, here we started with 15 numbers and tallies in matrix are 14.

Matrices are more meaningful when they represent a single type of activity or work. Two matrices should be drawn for 30 min. discussion and 20 min. lecture, or 40 min. arithmetic and 20 min. social studies.

Using the Matrix

(1) To determine general aspects of classroom interaction

The observer has to develop a description of the classroom interaction from the matrix. He begins by reporting the different kinds of statements in terms of percentages. First percentage of tallies in each of the columns is computed. This is done by dividing each of the column totals, 1 through 10, by the total number of tallies in the matrix. This gives the proportion of the total interaction in the observed classroom situation found in each category. A similar procedure is used to determine the % age of total teacher talk that falls in each category. This is done by dividing the total of each category, 1 through 7 by sum of these seven categories. For ex., teacher has 105 tallies in columns 1-7. If 10 are in column 3, the 10 is divided by 105 and we find that the amount of teacher talk that falls in category 3 in approximately 9½ % of the total amount of teacher talk. The pattern of interaction which the teacher has used with the class is now evident.

	First							Second			
	1	2	3	4	5	6	7	8	9	10	Total
1	2	1									
2		5		2							
3			8								
4		1		18				1			
5					53	2					
6						3		1	1		
7							3			2	
8			2				2	26			
9	1							1	10		
10								1	1	1	
Total	3	7	10	20	55	5	5	30	12	3	150
Column%	2	4 ½	6 ½	13½	36½	3 ½	3 ½	20	8	2	

Teacher talk

Column 1–7=105

100 × (105 ÷ 150) = 70%

Student talk

Column 8–9= 42

100 × (42 ÷ 150) = 28%

Indirect (1– 4) ÷ Direct (5–7) = I D ratio

(40–65) = 0.62

Indirect (1–3) – Direct (6–7) = Revised I D ratio

20 ÷ 10 = 2.0

Columns	1st	2nd	3rd	4th	5th	6th	7th	8th	9th	10th	Total
Age	9.09	18.18	9,09	9.09	18.18	0	9.09	0	0	18.18	99.99

The Teacher talk 70% of the total time, the students talked 28% of the time. 2% of the time was spent in silence or confusion.

Using the matrix the observer will be able to identify those cells in which he has heavy build-ups of tallies as well as the cells in which there are no tallies. The matrix provides the observer with a convenient device for analysis of the summarised teacher pupils interaction data.

Interpreting matrix data

Interpretations are made on the basis of analysis of matrices that were built in the research program by Flanders and those by Amidon.

Statement belonging to category 1 is used very rarely in any teaching style, average time appearing to be less than 0.5% of the total time. Indirect teachers may use up to 0.5% while direct teachers use less than 0.1%. Little difference in the use of category 1 is found between direct and indirect teachers. Direct teachers use as much praise as indirect teachers. (Category 2-2 %)

A variety of system designed to analyse pupil-teacher interaction in the CR have been developed by Withal (1949), Anderson (1939), Smith (1960), Aschner (1959), Hughes *et. al.* (1959), Medley and Mitzel (1958), and Amidon and Flanders (1963).

One of the best known systems for examining verbal interactive classroom behaviour is Flanders(VICS), Verbal Interaction Category System (VICS) is based on the Flanders system, but has been further developed to overcome some limitations of that as well as other.

Systems: RCS (Richard Ober), ETCS (Equivalent Talk Category System), RCEAS are come of them.

Categories

Teacher initiated talk: 1. Presents information or opinion.

2. Gives direction

3. Asks narrow question

4. Asks broad question.

Teacher response: 5. Accepts (a) ideas (b) behaviour (c) feeling

6. Rejects (a) ideas (b) behaviour (c) feeling

Pupils response: 7.Responds to teacher (a) predictably (b) unpredictably

8. Responds to another pupil

Pupil initiated talk: 9. Initiates talk to teacher

10. Initiates talk to another pupil

11. Silence.

12. Confusion

Observation System (John B. Hough) →16 category system

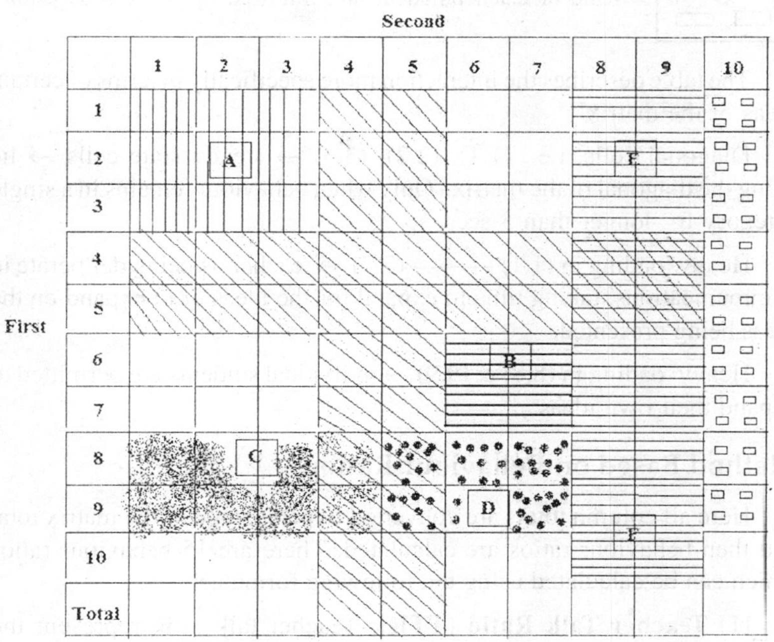

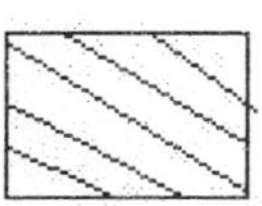

= Content cross (lecture, teacher questions)

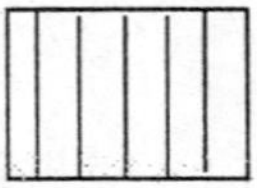
A= Extended indirect influence – use of extended indirect influence by the teacher

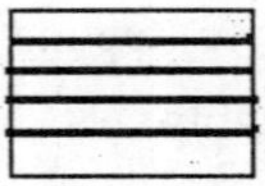
B = Extended direct influence – use of direct influence by teacher

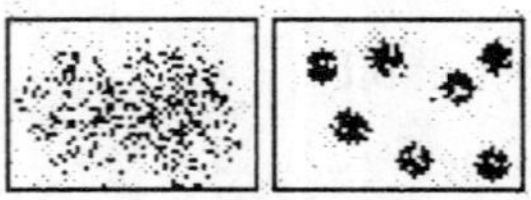
C&D = Teachers response to students comments

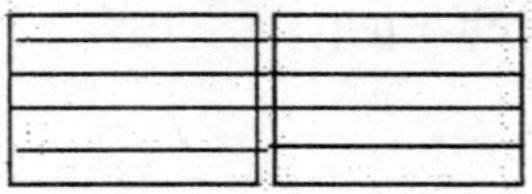
E&F = Students talk following Teacher talk

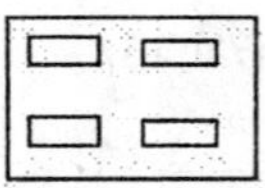
= Kind of teacher/student talk followed by silence/confusion

The table describes the interaction more specifically in terms of certain areas of the matrix.

Diagonal cells, i.e., (1,1), (2,2), (3,3) → steady state cells → lie along the diagonal of the matrix. Only when behaviour remains in a single category for longer than 3 secs.

Heavy loading in (1,1) ——— (7,7) → teacher is being deliberate in communications, taking time to expand for the ideas or to expand on the ideas being presented.

Heavy loading in (8,8) & (9,9) → individual students are permitted to expand their own ideas.

Method Based on Behaviour Ration

Here all column totals are converted to percentage of the matrix total and then behaviour ratios are calculated. There are 15 behaviour ratios which can be calculated using the following formulae

(1) Teacher Talk Ratio (TTR): Teacher talk ratio represent the performance of a teacher in terms of actions reflecting the tendency of teacher talk.

1 → frequencies belonging to category 1

$$TT = \frac{1+2+3+4+5+6+7}{N} \times 100$$

2

3

;

7 ———————— 7

(2) Indirect Teacher Talk Ratio (ITTR): Represents the performance of a teacher in terms of the actions encouraging and supporting pupil participation.

$$ITT = \frac{1+2+3+4}{N} \times 100$$

(3) Direct Teacher Talk Ratio (DTTR): Represents the performance of a teacher in term of action restricting student's participation.

$$DTT = \frac{5+6+7}{N} \times 100$$

(4) Pupil Talk Ratio (PTR): Refers to the verbal activities of the pupil (in response to the teacher)

$$PT = \frac{(8+9) \times 100}{N}$$

(5) Silence or Confusion Ratio (SCR): Represents silence or confusion.

$$SC = \frac{10 \times 100}{N}$$

1	Teacher Talk Ratio	Represents the performance of the teacher		
2	Pupil Talk Ratio	PTR	19	21
3	Silence/Confusion Ratio	SCR	11	12
4	Teacher Response Ratio	TRR	35	26
5	Teacher Question Ratio	TQR	20	19
6	Pupil Initiation Ratio	PIR	15	12
7	Steady State Ratio	SSR	52	46

8	Pupil Steady State Ratio	PSSR	26	37
9	Content Cross Ratio	CCR	68	72
10	Instantaneous Teacher Response Ratio	TRR-89	67	48
11	Instantaneous Teacher Question Ratio	TQR-89	39	42

Norms may be termed to be effective. While teacher exhibiting greater values of behaviour ratio in Sl.No. 1,3,7,9 &10 may be termed as ineffective teacher.

Indirect to Direct Ratio (I/D Ratio):

$$I/D=\frac{(1+2+3+4)}{5+6+7}\times 100$$

(6) Revised I/D Ratio: Next the observer focuses on relative number of indirect and direct teacher students. The total tallies in column 1,2,3,and 4 is divided by column 5,6 and 7 to find ID ratio, i.e., ratio of indirect to direct teacher statements. ID Ratio of 1.0 means, for every indirect statement there was one direct statement. ID ratio of 2.0 means for every two indirect statements there was only 1 direct statement etc.

Revised ID ratio finds the kind of emphasis given to motivation and control in a C.R. Tallies in column 1,2,and 3 in ÷ by number of tallies in columns 6 and 7 to find revised ratio. Categories1,2,3,6 and 7 are concerned with motivation and control and less concerned with actual presentation of subject matter. This ratio eliminates the effects of categories 4 and 5, and gives evidence whether the teacher is direct or indirect in his approach to motivation and control.

(7) Pupil Initiation Ratio (PIR): Represents pupils talk judged by the observer to be an act of initiation

$$PIR=\frac{(1+2+3)}{(8+9)}$$

(8) Teacher Response Ratio (TRR): Is an index of teacher's tendency to the ideas and feelings of students:

$$TRR=\frac{(1+2+3)}{(1+2+3+6)}\times 100$$

(9) Teacher Question Ratio (TQR): Represents the teacher behaviour involving the use of questions while guiding more content oriented part of the class discussion

$$\frac{(4)}{(4+5)}\times 100$$

(10) Content Cross Ratio: Indicates the extract to which discussion was found on the subject matter. It shows the proportion of the classroom activity related to the teachers question and lecturing w.r.t his total classroom interaction.

$$\text{CCR} = \frac{4+5}{\text{N}}\times 100$$

(11) Steady State Ratio: SSR: It indicates the tendency of teacher and Pupil talk to remain in the same state for a period longer than three seconds.

$$\text{SSR} = \frac{\text{Total frequencie s of steady state cells}}{\text{N}}\times 100$$

(12) Pupil Steady Ratio (PSSR): indicates the tendency of pupils talk to remain in the same state for a period longer 3 seconds.

$$\text{PSSR} = \frac{(8,8)+(9,9)}{(8+9)}\times 100$$

(13) Instantaneous Teacher Response Ratio: (TRR-89) Index of the teacher's tendency to praise or integrate pupil ideas and feelings into the class discussion, when pupil stops talking

$$\text{TR} - 89\frac{(8,1)+(8,2)+(8,3)+(9,1)+(9,2)+(9,3)}{(8,1)+(8,2)+(8,3)+(8,6)+(8,7)+(9,1)+(9,2)+(9,3)+(9,6)+(9,7)}$$

(14) Instantaneous Teacher Question Ratio: (TQR-89) Indicates tendency of teacher to respond to pupil talk with question based on his own ideas composed to his tendency to teacher

$$\text{TQR} - 89 = \frac{(8,4)+(9,4)}{[(8,4)+(8,5)]+[(9,4)+(9,5)]}$$

(15) Interpretation of Behaviour Ratios: Behaviour has to be interpreted against the norms, i.e., the standard normative expectations. Flanders developed these norms for various grades in USA. They have also been developed in Indian condition.

Table: Behaviour Ratio Norms

Sl.No	*Behaviour Ratio*	*Sym-bol*	*Flan-ders*	*Indian condition*
1	Teacher Talk	TT	70	67
2	Pupil Talk	PT	19	21
3	Silence/Confusion	SC	11	12
4	Teacher Response Ratio	TRR	35	26
5	Teacher Question ratio	TQR	20	19
6	Pupil Initiation Ratio	PIR	15	12
7	Steady State Ratio	SSR	52	46
8	Pupil Steady State Ratio	PSSR	26	37
9	Content Cross Ratio	CCR	68	72
10	Instantaneous Teacher Response Ratio	TRR-89	67	48
11	Instantaneous Teacher Question Ratio	TQR-89	39	42
12	Instantaneous Teacher Question Ratio	TQR-89	39	42

Teacher exhibiting greater values of behaviour rotation Sl.No 2, 4,5,6,8 and 11 than the norms may be termed to be effective. While teacher exhibiting greater values of behaviour ratio in Sl.No 1,3,7,9,and 10 may be termed as ineffective teacher.

Specimen matrix of a teacher

Category	1	2	3	4	5	6	7	8	9	10	Total
1	1	22	5	1	8	4	1	24	-	-	66
2	1	68	3	4	5	5	5	324	1	17	433
3	-	1	26	2	2	3	1	82	1	2	120
4	1	25	6	360	6	3	1	4	3	3	412
5	3	32	18	2	365	14	1	11	2	2	450
6	2	42	7	15	8	29	1	18	1	-	123
7	-	3	-	2	-	8	11	8	-	1	33
8	57	219	53	20	55	55	11	871	6	9	1326
9	-	3	1	3	1	-	-	7	7	-	22
10	1	18	1	3	-	2	1	7	1	27	61
Total	66	433	120	412	450	123	33	1356	22	61	
% age	2.15	14.08	3.90	13.4	14.6	3.99	1.07	44.08	0.7	1.98	

Matrix-Total: 3076

The matrix of this teacher reveals that he uses more of elaborative lecture, as the cell (5, 5) has 365 tallies which is slightly more than cell (4, 4) (6, 6) → low → teacher uses very little direction or rarely discusses in his CR teaching.

(2, 5) → 32 tallies → Teacher elaborates his lecture by asking narrow question. 68 narrow questions are asked of which 32 were utilised for elaboration of lecture.

% age of teacher talk is 53.21 % which is significantly below the average amount of teacher talk. (Norms of teacher talk - 68%)

That of pupil is 44.81 % above average for the amount of pupil talk. (20% norms)

Only 1.98 % pupil tallies pupil initiated.

The teacher is more indirect as compared to direct as I./D ratio is 0.608.

Among the cells which have more than 3 hundred tallies, 3 are steady state cell (4,4), (5,5), (8,8) and there are transitory cells, (8-2), (2-8) (3-8). This indicates that Q-R types of pattern prevailed in the classes of this teacher.

Objectives of Flander's Category System

The main objectives are

- To identify teacher's behaviour in the class through interaction analysis
- To collect the objective data and systematic record of the teacher behaviour by this method.
- To formulate remedial strategies with reference to the teaching methods.

Assumptions of Flander's Category System

- The classroom environment is most important in the entire learning process.
- Teacher's behaviour influences the teaching very much.
- Democratic behaviour in the classroom is highly appreciated.
- The classroom behaviour can be changed by using feedback.
- The observation of the teacher's classroom behaviour is possible objectively.
- The mutual relationship between the pupil and the teacher carries much importance.

– Verbal behaviour can be observed more reliably than the non-verbal behaviour.

Advantages of Flander's Interaction Analysis Technique

The value of Flander's technique in the field of understanding the dynamics of teaching learning process in terms of interaction between a teacher and his pupils has been recognized by researchers. A large number of studies have been conducted in different countries during the past few years in which FIAT has been employed with advantage.

The advantages of FIAT may be summarized as below –

(1) It is a reliable and objective technique of observing and analysing the verbal behaviour of a teacher and classroom interaction. With the help of this systematic and objective feedback may be given to improve teaching effectiveness and meaningful classroom interaction.

(2) It helps in determining the pattern and flow of teaching behaviour.

(3) It helps in analysing the classroom activities.

(4) FIAT provides of valuable feedback to teachers. It can be used as an effective pre-training and post-training measure. Through the use of this system, student teachers may practice and learn much desirable teaching behaviour.

(5) This method adds and supplements teaching techniques like simulated and micro-teaching.

(6) FIAT can be used as a major tool in in-service and pre-service education programmes. All trainees could learn interaction analysis and than use it to attain individual self-improvement goals which can be selected by each participant. Being a potential tool of feedback, it helps in acquiring desirable patterns of teaching and modifying one's teaching behaviour.

(7) It is an effective instrument to measure the social-emotional environment of the class.

(8) Even though the trainer is not present in the class, a picture of the interaction that occurred in the class can be drawn with the help of the matrix.

(9) It is possible for a teacher to make an audio/video recording of self-taught lessons and evaluate his behaviour. Thus he may be freed from the anxiety and pressures of being observed by others.

(10) It is a tool which assists the teacher in planning strategies by providing a set of categories and suggesting means of organising patterns of instruction. If the teacher is familiar with the system, he would

intentionally teacher to use some behaviour categories which form desirable and successful pattern of instruction.

(11) It may help as a research tool in this field of teacher education. Research in areas of teaching, teacher behaviour, classroom environment and management, teaching methods and strategies, pre-service and service education of teachers could be carried out using FIAT.

EXERCISES

1. What is Interaction teaching?
2. Briefly explain the Flanders System of Interaction Analysis.
3. State the advantages of Flanders' Interaction Analysis.

Chapter 4

Strategies of Teaching

Objectives

After reading this unit, you should be able to:

- Explain teaching strategy
- List out types of teaching strategies
- Explain the advantages of brainstorming
- Describe sensitivity training
- Spot sensitivity training sessions
- Explain the causes insensitivity
- State modular approach in teaching
- Explain book format modules

INTRODUCTION

Meaning of Teaching Strategy

The term teaching or instructional strategy stands for the type of strategy used by the teacher in carrying out his teaching or instructional work. The word strategy in its etymological derivation owes its origin from a Greek work '*strategia*' and may be defined as plans and specific ways devised and employed for the realisation of a goal. According to the Callin's English Gem Dictionary, 1968 the strategy means the art of war or the skill of war. In encyclopedia, its meaning has been given as an art of deploying army, so that a specific goal can be achieved. Hence, according to encyclopedia, "strategy I the science of art of planning and directing large military movements and operations." Strategy is such planning or line of action which is related to the working system. In other words, strategy is that skilful planning of a working system by which the objective can be achieved conveniently. Strategies are never the same. These change according to the changing situations.

Strategy as a term is quite in vogue in Military Science and Warfare. Here it stands for the effective plans, means and ways derived and employed for winning a war. A chess player may also be said to employ effective strategies for winning his game. The word strategy is being used in with reference to wars but for the last few years, it is also be used by the social scientists in social planning, human dynamics and teaching areas.

B.D. Smith defines the term strategy as "The term strategy refers to pattern of acts that serve to attain certain outcomes and to guard against certain others."

A teacher may need to use of strategies for carrying out his task of teaching as effectively as possible. Teaching is a purposeful activity performed by the teacher for guiding, directing and showing the right path to the learners in their pursuit for the realisation of the set teaching-learning objectives. Thinking in this way, we may define the term teaching strategy as below, "Teaching or instructional strategies may well stand for plans, means and specific ways especially devised and employed by the teachers for guiding, directing and showing path to the learners for the realisation of the set instructional or teaching-learning objectives".

According to Stones and Morrison, "Teaching strategy is a generalised plan for a lesson which includes structured desired learner behaviour in terms of goals of instruction and an outline of planned tactics necessary to implement the strategy."

- The analysis of this definition reveals that: Teaching strategy stands for a generalised plan, ways and means for carrying out the task of teaching, i.e., more specifically for teaching a particular lesson.
- Teaching work is directed towards the realisation of the set teaching-learning objectives.
- Teaching strategy is devised and employed for helping the learners in the realisation of the set teaching-learning objectives.
- Teaching strategy brings out a scheme, programme or teaching-learning structure, which if followed may help in the better realisation of the set teaching-learning objectives.

- Teaching strategy requires a number of well planned tactics for its effective implementation, i.e., teaching tactics are the essential components of a teaching strategy.
- Teaching, teaching-learning structure set through a teaching strategy may be represented by this diagram.
  (i) A teaching strategy is devised and employed for enabling the learner to realise the set teaching-learning objectives.
  (ii) A teaching strategy is always devised and employed in the light of the needs, interests and abilities of the learner, the facilities and learning environment available to the learner for carrying out his efforts for learning and the pre-fixed learning objectives.
  (iii) Teaching strategy remains open for further modification and improvement in the light of the feedback received from the learner.
  (iv) Teaching-learning objectives make central point and goal of the teaching-learning structure. These are also dynamic and not static. We can bring desirable modification in the objectives in the light of the feedback received from the learners, teaching-learning environment and teaching strategies.

By using self-pacing techniques, instructors do not have to expend time providing cognitive information to students, The package provides the information while the instructor works with small groups or individual students to help clarify and build beyond the basic concepts. Through this approach the learner is able to pace his own learning and make use of as little or as much instruction as he may need from the instructional packages and instructors, so that he can master a set of objectives at the rate that best fits his learning style.

Teaching Strategies

Institutions of higher learning across the nation are responding to political, economic, social and technological pressures to be more responsive to students' needs and more concerned about how well students are prepared to assume future societal roles. Faculty are already feeling the pressure to lecture less, to make learning environments more interactive, to integrate technology into the learning experience, and to use collaborative learning strategies when appropriate.

Instructional Methods Information

Instructional methods and teaching methods mean the same thing. They are primarily descriptions of the learning objective–oriented activities and flow of information between teachers and students. Although some may argue otherwise, to split hairs over whether such methods are meaningfully different adds nothing to the process of learning to be a teacher. Direct and indirect instruction are two main categories that many educators find useful for classifying teaching methods, but it is, as you will see, a bit more complicated than placing all instruction into two categories. Any instructional method a teacher uses has advantages, disadvantages and requires some preliminary preparation. Often times, a particular teaching method will naturally flow into another, all within the same lesson, and excellent teachers have developed the skills to make the process seamless to the students. Which instructional method is "right" for a particular lesson depends on many things, and among them are the age and developmental level of the students, what the students already know, and what they need to know to succeed with the lesson, the subject-matter content, the objective of the lesson, the available people, time, space and material resources and the physical setting. Another, more difficult problem is to select an instructional method that best fits one's particular teaching style and the lesson-situation. There is no one "right" method for teaching a particular lesson, but there are some criteria that pertain to each that can help a teacher make the best decision possible.

Types of Teaching Strategies

Teachers may use different types of strategies in different teaching-learning situations for the realisation (achieving) of teaching objectives. These strategies may be broadly classified as: (i) autocratic teaching strategies (content centered and teacher dominated) (ii) Democratic teaching strategies (student oriented and democratically organised).

Autocratic Strategies	Democratic Strategies
1. Lecture strategy	1. Discussion strategy
2. Demonstration strategy	2. Question – Answer strategy.
3. Tutorial strategy.	3. Discovery/Heuristic strategy.
4. Narration strategy.	4. Problem solving strategy.
5. Description strategy.	5. Project strategy
6. Explanation strategy.	6. Independent study strategy.
7. Illustration strategy.	7. Homework or assignment strategy.
8. Programmed instruction strategy.	8. Drill/Practice work strategy.
9. Role-playing strategy.	9. Excursion strategy.

	10. A-v aids employed strategy. 11. Brainstorming strategy. 12. Sensitivity training strategy. 13. Computer associated instruction strategy.

A tactic may be described as a goal-linked influencing behaviour of the teacher–the way a teacher behaves in the instructional situation to achieve a goal. A tactic is, therefore, a short-term device and it may range from one question or statement to a complex or verbal or purposeful non-verbal teacher behaviour interlaced with student behaviour.

Tactical Concepts	**Strategic Concepts**
1. They are reflected even in a short-terminstructional sequence.	1. They are reflected in longer instructional units.
2. Tactical concepts form part of strategic concepts.	2. Strategic concepts have wide scope. They include tactical concepts.
3. The number of tactical concepts is very large.	3. Number is very small.
4. The tactical concepts may change from moment to moment.	4. Strategic concepts have wider application.
5. Tactics require presence of mind.	5. Strategic concepts require thinking at deeper level.
6. Tactical concepts are situational in nature.	6. Strategic concepts are designed not on the spot, but before the emergence of a situation.
7. Tactical concepts are studied through episodes, incidents, cycles and behaviour episodes.	7. They are studied through complex chains, teaching modules and ventures.

Four sequential units are employed for the study of tactical concepts.

(a) Episode (b) Incidents

(c) Teaching cycles (d) Behaviour episodes.

(a) Episode: It may be defined as one or more exchanges which comprise a complete verbal transaction between the teacher and the learner. An episodes has 3 phases:

(1) An 'opening' phase: of an episode consists of verbal moves in the form of a remark or remarks like question to the learners.

(2) The 'continuing' or 'sustaining' phase: of an episode consists of verbal moves (remarks) which are in the form o replies or responses to the questions, claims, comments or opinions, discussions etc.

(3) The 'terminal phase': of an episode consists of verbal moves (remarks) which serve expertly to cut off the flow of discussion or supplementary or elaborate comments.

(b) Incidents: An incident differs from an episode that it is conceived of as a contextual unit which is question-centered rather than topic centered. It may be noted that the boundaries of episode and incident may coincide.

(c) Teaching cycles: Consists of four types of verbal or pedagogical moves: Structuring, Soliciting, Responding and Reacting.

(d) Behaviour episodes: Consists of a unit of time wherein the individual is going in one direction. There may not involve interaction among 2 or more classroom participants.

Lecture: For many years, the lecture method was the most widely used instructional strategy in college classrooms. Nearly 80% of all U.S. college classrooms in the late 1970s reported using some form of the lecture method to teach students (Cashin, 1990). Although the usefulness of other teaching strategies is being widely examined today, the lecture still remains an important way to communicate information.

Used in conjunction with active learning-teaching strategies, the traditional lecture can be an effective way to achieve instructional goals. The advantages of the lecture approach are that it provides a way to communicate a large amount of information to many listeners, maximises instructor control and is non-threatening to students. The disadvantages are that lecturing minimises feedback from students, assumes an unrealistic level of student understanding and comprehension, and often disengages students from the learning process causing information to be quickly forgotten.

The following recommendations can help make the lecture approach more effective (Cashin, 1990):

1. Fit the lecture to the audience
2. Focus your topic - remember you cannot cover everything in one lecture
3. Prepare an outline that includes 5-9 major points you want to cover in one lecture

4. Organize your points for clarity
5. Select appropriate examples or illustrations
6. Present more than one side of an issue and be sensitive to other perspectives
7. Repeat points when necessary
8. Be aware of your audience - notice their feedback
9. Be enthusiastic - you don't have to be an entertainer but you should be excited by your topic. (Cashin, 1990, pp. 60-61)

LECTURE

Advantages	Disadvantages	Preparation
Factual material is presented in a direct, logical manner. May provide experiences that inspire– useful for large groups.	Proficient oral skills are necessary. Audience is often passive. Learning is difficult to gauge. Communi-cation is one-way. Not appropriate for children below grade 4.	There should be a clear introduction and summ-ary.Effectiveness related to time and scope of content. Is always audience specific; often incl-udes examples, anecdotes.

LECTURE WITH DISCUSSION

Advantages	Disadvantages	Preparation
Involves students, at least after the lecture. Students can ques-tion, clarify and chall-enge. Lecture can be inters-persed with discussion.	Time constraints may affect discussion oppor-tunities. Effectiveness is connected to approp-riate questions and discussion; often re-quires teacher to "shift gears" quickly.	Teacher should be pre-pared to allow ques-tions during lecture, as approp-riate. Teacher should also anticipate difficult ques-tions and prepare appro-priate responses in advance.

PANEL OF EXPERTS

Advantages	Disadvantages	Preparation
Experts present different opini-ons. Can provoke better discu-ssion than a one person discu-ssion. Frequent change of speaker keeps attention from lagging.	Personalities may over-shadow content. Experts are often not effective speakers. Subject may not be in logical order. Not appropriate for elementary age stude-nts.Logistics can be troublesome.	Teacher coordinates focus of panel, intro-duces and summa-rizes.Teacher briefs panel.

Discussion: There are a variety of ways to stimulate discussion. For example, some faculty begin a lesson with a whole group discussion to refresh students' memories about the assigned reading(s). Other faculty finds it helpful to have student's list critical points or emerging issues, or generate a set of questions stemming from the assigned reading(s). These strategies can also be used to help focus large and small group discussions.

Obviously, a successful class discussion involves planning on the part of the instructor and preparation on the part of the students. Instructors should communicate this commitment to the students on the first day of class by clearly articulating course expectations. Just as the instructor carefully plans the learning experience, the students must comprehend the assigned reading and show up for class on time, ready to learn.

DISCUSSION

Advantages	Disadvantages	Preparation
Pools ideas and exper-iences from groups Effective after a presen-tation, film or exper-ience that needs to be analysed. Allows ever-yone to participate in an active process	Not practical with more that 20 students. A few students can dominate. Some stud-ents may not parti-cipate. Is time consu-ming. Can get off the track	Requires careful planning by teacher to guide discu-ssion. Requires question outline

SMALL GROUP DISCUSSION

Advantages	Disadvantages	Preparation
Allows for participation of everyone. Students often are more comfortable in small groups. Groups can reach consensus.	Needs careful thought as to purpose of group. Groups may get sidetracked.	Need to prepare specific tasks or questions for group to answer.

The Drill Strategy

Method of implementation

1. Set the scene
2. Check meaning and understanding
3. Emphasise key learning points
4. Drill
5. Written test
6. Marking and recording

Overview

- the method of teaching through repetition
- aims to produce an automatic response (rote)
- continual reinforcement until knowledge is automatically triggered by key words to respondent
- may be ineffective if implementation is allowed to become dull and boring to students
- at risk of no or little understanding from students
- effective if material being taught is understood by learners

The Demonstration Strategy

Method of implementation

1. Set the scene
2. Explain and demonstrate the skill/content

3. Student practice with teacher feedback
4. Apply/transfer skill/content in another context

Overview

- aims to promote acquisition of new skills through observation and imitation
- used to help develop thinking skills and problem solving skills
- commonly used in subjects such as, PE, Handwriting, Spelling, Music etc
- does not promote individual learning
- the implementation is crucial, maintaining interest and enthusiasm at all times

A Group Discussion Strategy

Method of implementation: 1. Organise the group 2. Set the task 3. Discussion 4. Presentation of findings

Overview

- major purpose is to foster and enhance communication skills within the class
- helps promote thinking and decision making skills as well as fostering different viewpoints and opinions
- may be used in all key areas of learning
- major limitation is that it is generally not suitable for younger levels because of the level of reasoning required in order for it to work
- is dependent upon the group routines and social climate of the class
- teachers must be able to guide and give aid as necessary but the class environment and the groups themselves often determine the outcomes

The Guided Discovery Strategy

Method of implementation

1. The teacher sets a problem
2. The students explore the problem
3. Teacher and students discuss the problem and formulate conclusions

Overview

- major purpose is to have students actively involved in their own learning and problem solving
- most suited to subjects that require active learning practices, concept development and discovering the solution to problems
- it is effective in helping students to develop a better understanding of ideas and concepts
- mainly used with abstract concepts, however, concept materials are beneficial, especially for younger students
- major disadvantage is that it is not suitable for teaching a large number of facts in a concise and efficient manner
- without correct teacher-guidance, students are at risk of learning incorrect information
- not suited to students of all levels

It is highly recommended that you refer to the text referenced below for a more detailed view of the strategies outlined here. Always bear in mind that teaching strategies are not exclusive to one another and that the teacher who is open to furthering their skills in passing on information to their students, is the teacher that will ultimately cope better, and benefit their students the most.

Some examples of teacher strategies

- Have students monitor their own learning and thinking (Example: have student monitor a peer's learning/thinking/behaving in dyad)
- Have students learn study strategies (e.g., SQ3R, SQ4R)
- Have students make predictions about information to be presented next based on what they have read
- Have students relate ideas to existing knowledge structures (Important to have relevant knowledge structures well learned)
- Have students develop questions; ask questions of themselves, about what's going on around them (Have you asked a good question today?)
- Help students to know when to ask for help (must be able to self-monitor; require students to show how they have attempted to deal with the problem of their own)
- Show students how to transfer knowledge, attitudes, values, skills to other situations or tasks

BRAINSTORMING

Advantages	Disadvantages	Preparation
Listening exercise that allows creative thinking for new ideas. Encourages full participation because all ideas are equally recorded. Draws on group's knowledge and experience. Spirit of cooperation is created. One idea can spark off other ideas.	Can be unfocused. Needs to be limited to 5-7 minutes. Students may have difficulty getting away from known reality. If not managed well, criticism and negative evaluation may occur. Value to students depends in part on their maturity level.	Teacher selects issue. Teacher must be ready to intervene when the process is hopelessly bogged down.

ROLE PLAYING

Advantages	Disadvantages	Preparation
Introduces problem situation dramatically. Provides opportunity for students to assume roles of others and thus appreciate another point of view. Allows for exploration of solutions. Provides opportunity to practice skills.	Some students may be too self-conscious. Not appropriate for large groups. Some students may feel threatened.	Teacher has to define problem situation and roles clearly. Teacher must give very clear instructions

Sensitivity Training

Sensitivity Training: A brainwashing technique (also called Relational Therapy)

Traditional psychology involves two persons — the patient on the couch and the psychologist in the armchair. Now people with things troubling their minds meet in groups to "talk, walk, cry, comfort, touch, feel etc". Very few of the people who become involved in these group sessions actually realise what is taking place. The truth is that they have become involved in sensitivity training, a clever psychological technique and tool for producing change.

Sensitivity Training is really a form of brainwashing, originated by the communists and refined and renamed for American consumption. The Russian Scientist, Pavlov, whose experiments with the behavior of dogs and the methods of controlling their actions and reactions seems to have influenced Lenin's philosophy of controlling people through the psychological manipulations of the mind. This whole theory, or course, is based on the unscriptural, animalistic, evolutionary concept of man and it has been used for years by the communists – both Russian and Chinese— to bind their people in mental and physical slavery.

Sensitivity Training in the United States apparently had its beginning about 1946, with the formation of the National Training Laboratories in Group Development. In 1947, the name was changed to the National Training Laboratories Institute for Applied Behavioral Science under the auspices of the National Educational Association Adult Education Service. In 1962, it became a separate division of NEA, and in 1967, it became an independent nonprofit corporation associated with the National Education Association. This relationship is important to understand, since every effort is being made to make Sensitivity Training Mandatory for all public schools. The NEA alone is one of the prime promoters of Sex Education in the public schools and there is a definite relationship between Sex Education and Sensitivity Training.

A very simple definition of Sensitivity Training is: "Psychological techniques and programs designed to change the standards, attitudes and behaviour of individuals".

The term "Sensitivity Training" was apparently coined by behavioral scientists who are obsessed with the idea that a Utopian society and world can be realised through psychological means.

Sensitivity Training goes by many different names to deceive the unwary. Sensitivity training techniques have always been presented under a variety of names, but with the recent exposures of the true nature and character of sensitivity training, the proliferation of names is astounding. Here are some of the names under which sensitivity training now masquerades:

– Reality Therapy
– Conflict Management
– New Consciousness
– Psycho-drama
– Developing Personal Potential
– Feeling Therapy
– Nude Therapy
– Interpersonal Relations
– Group Development
– Group Therapy

- Group Theory
- Group Dynamics
- Group Discussion
- Interpersonal Behaviour
- Self-evolution
- Auto-criticism
- Basic Encounter Group
- Human Potential Workshop
- Cybernetics
- Family Life Education
- Cursillo Movements
- Enhancement of Human Potential
- Management Development
- Sociometry
- Self-honesty Sessions
- Group Life Institute
- Gestalt Therapy
- Social Psychology
- Actualisation Groups
- Sensory Awareness Groups
- Social Philosophy
- Human Relations Lab
- Personal Development Lab
- Group Confession
- Interpersonal Competence
- Conflict Resolution
- T-group Training
- Prayer Therapy
- Operant Conditioning
- Synanon Games Club
- Mind Set
- Body Awareness
- Community Relations
- Leadership Class
- Socio-drama
- Truth Sessions
- Micro-labs
- Team Interpretation
- Role Playing
- Confrontation Groups
- Sensory Playing
- Growth Groups
- Personality Evaluation
- Gut Level Talks

Of course, not everything presented under these titles is sensitivity training, but when you see any of these names, it will bear investigation.

What is the real purpose of Sensitivity Training?

Proponents of this technique claim that it will increase love and trust, open up honest communication, develop leadership and produce greater understanding and sensitivity for the feelings of others. Who could find fault with such noble goals?

Sensitivity training involves group confession where the individual's problems become the problems of the group, which in turn tries to find a solution. After criticising others and being criticised you. Doubt is introduced into the mind of each individual as to whose standards are really proper.

How to Spot Sensitivity Training Sessions?

We have already pointed out that you can't go by the name "Sensitivity Training" alone. In addition, not every sensitivity training session will use the exact same techniques. The following methods are given only because they are perhaps the most frequently used and readily observable procedures:

1. One or more people in the group, known technically as trainers or change agents or facilitators, will give the impression that they are merely stimulating free expression or openness, but will actually be manipulating the group, without their knowledge, if possible.
2. Most sensitivity training sessions stress agreement upon certain ground rules, which actually become the first foundation of sensitivity training, since individuals hesitate to break rules which they themselves agreed to at the outset. Such rules may simply be agreeing to stay until the session is ended; agreeing to be open and honest in all conversations; agreeing not to talk during non-verbal exercises; and in some cases, the rules go so far as to agree not to object to language normally thought objectionable in the group.
3. You will probably be asked to speak of or write out your greatest problems or faults or hang-ups so the group can make suggestions as to how you can overcome these things. You in turn, may be encouraged to criticise others in the group if you feel they are not fully open or honest in confessing their faults.
4. Non-verbal exercises may be used where individuals are asked to convey their feelings by some means other than words. This may involve the use of the eyes, facial expression, or body movement, including touching each others hands, faces, or bodies in an effort to communicate feeling.
5. Periods of silence and meditation with eyes either closed or open are frequently used when the discussions seem to be developing in the wrong way or when the trainer desires to make an abrupt change in the procedures.
6. Marathon sessions are frequently used to break down "inhibitions" and encourage participants to express "their true feelings" under the stress of physical fatigue and lack of sleep.
7. Body awareness exercises are often used, such as the group pushing a person down to help him feel hostility, and then helping him up to

help him feel love. Or a person may be asked to fall backward, only to be caught by members of the group, to develop trust. All of those techniques involve bodily contact in one form or another.

WHAT IS SENSITIVITY?

Respondent's outlook on what sensitivity is varies considerably. Some believed that sensitivity is in fact a sort of native talent. It has a lot to do with personality traits that you are born with. Others believed that sensitivity is something which is not so much developed, as allowed to exist. It's called "empathy", and it's a trait that isn't so much developed as allowed to exist. Many things in our modern world tend to cause us to believe that we shouldn't empathise.

WHAT CAUSES INSENSITIVITY?

What is responsible for sensitivity problems?

Respondents felt that problems might be associated with self-absorbtion. Well, I have this problem; it comes from being so wound up with my own problems that I don't "have time" for others Don't know if this is your sticking point, but, if it is, it shows in the tension you project. Semi-silly idea; ask a friend to unobtrusively follow you around with a camcorder and take candid shots of you in public. This would probably be very difficult to implement (too much "camera awareness") but you could really see how you present yourself to others. I've already found that I've acted inconsistent in cases where I told myself I wanted to pay attention to someone I could care less about, and it showed. "Sigh"

A lack of self-honesty was also blamed.

Playing games with oneself will surely cause problems in dealing with others.

BE PREPARED

Keeping an open mind prepares you to be sensitive to others.

Keeping a VERY open mind helps. You have to always be on your toes, trying to relate to what the person is saying, even though you may not have experienced what they have.

SENSITIVITY AS A SKILL

Most respondents believed that sensitivity to others could be developed.

Some people DO have this ability, but most just fake it. It comes with experience....

People learn from their experiences and make judgements based upon these. If certain behaviour results in favourable responses, we tend to repeat it. Given unfavorable responses, we tend not to repeat it (at least, not very often). So any sense of "prediction" is mainly the application of past experience.

LISTENING

One frequently discussed "technique" was listening.

The trick was to listen more carefully to people. We should be caught up in a little world of our own, and when we hear a key word that related to something that was in our little world, then jump in the conversation.

Suggestions for effective listening techniques were made

Listening is an interactive activity. As you learn how to communicate immediacy, the rest begins to come more and more easily. For example, as you are listening to someone, try to understand not just what they are saying but why they are saying it. Then, as you start to guess, ask questions which indicate an interest not just in the what, but the why. You will probably be wrong most of the time, but by asking, you don't have to guess. The other person can tell you if you understand or not. It takes some practice, but it is well worth it!

HOW TO LISTEN?

- Look directly at the other person. Don't look away at other things, no matter how distracting.
- Nod in agreement occasionally – if nothing else, this will keep the other person talking – better still to do it at the right places
- Completely regain from trying to insert a comment of your own. (I have trouble with this, and tend to trample conversations, because if I don't say it I'll forget what I want to say in trying to listen to the rest of the conversation).

- Lean towards the other person just a little (too much can look confrontational). These things will convince the other person that you're listening. As long as you stay focused on him/her and don't try to butt in, you'll be able to listen and really hear what they're saying. "Thus it is better to be silent and thought a fool than to open one's mouth and remove all doubt." Waiting till the other person finished is polite and it gives you time to compose an answer, rather than blurt out something.
- Listen – listen very carefully, look into their eyes, don't let outside things interrupt your concentration on what they are saying. If you don't understand exactly what they said ask questions and get them to go over things. Summarise what they have told you. Don't always offer advice–its not always wanted – often a sympathetic ear is just enough. The important thing is to show the other person that you are willing to drop all outside distractions and to focus on their needs for a while—to show you care for them and they will likewise return the favour when needed.

Another suggestion was to literally take notes, whenever practicable. This was also recommended as it tends to build up the mental note taking habit.

NON-VERBAL COMMUNICATION

Acquiring an understanding of non-verbal communication was recommended.

People say so much, their gestures, looks, and body language in general. Even the way they build sentences is different when they are happy or sad. Sometimes it is obvious, sometimes you have to know them for a while. That's one part of it. The other is using this information.

Touch was suggested as a way of "testing the waters."

There's a good way to know if someone is ready for your friendship. Find an excuse and touch their hand. You can lie and you can keep your face calm, but few people can stand a touch from someone they don't like.

Looking at the way people are acting gives an indication of their feelings, too.

Watching people helps. If you have known someone for a long period of time and watch how they behave, then eventually if they start doing things that are "out of character", you are better at picking that up.

DEVELOPING TRUST AND ENCOURAGING OPENNESS

Getting the other person to feel comfortable with you is a critical need. This is your responsibility. Most people are more open than one may think, if they feel comfortable with it, so you have to give them that feeling.

Trust is the key to openness.

The major word is trust. Once you've won someone's trust and respect they open to you. But a trust is easy to loose too. And if you loose someone's trust you can never get it back.

Asking questions was heavily recommended for getting people to open up, even when on uncertain ground.

When you know SOMETHING is wrong, but have no idea what, bluff. Ask leading questions, like you know something already, but (be subtle).

Ask people about themselves. If someone finds out that you are actually interested in THEM, it is amazing how they will respond. You can ask questions about their family, about their work/school, or about everyday things, i.e., "Did anything exciting happen today/this week?" (and follow up – the standard response is "no"- I usually say "C'mon surely SOMETHING interesting happened.")

It was pointed out that it is critical to listen BEFORE asking questions, And to consider the impact of the question on the person asked.

At first, don't ask and just listen. Never ask if you at their place wouldn't like the question.

Be open yourself. Let people know how YOU feel.

Basically if you want to show people that you're sensitive to have to open yourself up to them as well.

Remember, NEVER assume anything. Sure, you can guess, but remember that you are only guessing. The main point, though, is to tell the other person how YOU feel.....

'You seem to be nervous... Are you?'

'You still seem to be upset, and that bothers me....'

'You know, I love it when you smile at me that way....'

'I really appreciate it when you do things like this......'

Best advice is to honestly care about other people. Then you can pick up their "vibes" almost naturally (since you care, you pay attention to what they like and dislike, and become aware of these things).

Be friendly, honest, and open, and you will develop the friendships you want. Be consistent, so that people can see you can be trusted, and they will begin to open up. Above all, be there when your friends need you.

USING YOUR OWN FEELINGS

Understanding the causes of uncomfortable feelings in yourself is helpful in understanding others, even if it means confronting unpleasant realities about yourself.

That's exactly the way how it works. If you get that (uncomfortable) feeling, try to find out what initiates it. Of course, it means thinking more about people. It helps a lot to talk with a really close friend about it. When you get that feeling while talking to him/here. Most people have this capability (if you like to describe it that way), think it is based on rational understanding your own feelings. The results are not always nice, because nobody is perfect. I mean, nobody likes to think about his bad properties, but doing so is the consequence. Once you started it, you can't run away.

SOME OTHER VALUABLE THINGS TO REMEMBER

Be open, yourself, and remember that

(1) Everybody is entitled to their feelings, no matter how illogical they are;

(2) There is no such thing as 'blame'… Everybody involved is equally at fault;

(3) Don't attack, but express – Not, 'You did this/that, 'but' I feel this/that';

(4) Don't leave a problem unresolved— it will just get worse with time;

(5) Nobody's perfect – not even you …

Sensitivity to the circumstances and feelings of others is the cornerstone of human relationships. The seasons of sunshine and joy and alternatively that of cold and suffering spare no mortal, the desperate need for caring and understanding from his fellow human beings. It is important to note that sensitivity is not just an emotion; it must express itself in actions as well, especially when people we know are experiencing pain and difficulties.

The first task in sensitivity training is to climb out of ourselves and notice others.

The next level is to respond which can take many forms. One size does not fit all and often the same situation at different times requires different approaches.

1. The first step in any interaction, especially in delicate situations, is to press the internal "pause button", i.e., not to shoot from the hip but to stop and think if what we are about to say is advisable.

2. Refrain from asking too many questions. Take your cue from the person in pain. People who are suffering find it especially offensive for someone who has not previously shown much interest in them to grill them on all of the gory details of their situation. It makes them feel like they are the object of curiosity and gossip.

3. Mishna advises that one "should not try to console a bereaved person while the remains of the deceased are still before them." When pain is so new and fresh, a person is not in a position where they can hear moralising comments such as "they lived a good, long life" or "left good children behind" etc. At this time these pronouncements are often premature. This is the time when the afflicted needs validation and affirmation. They will ask for perspective when they are ready.

4. Many have confided that people shunned them during their hour of suffering. One woman who was undergoing chemotherapy recalled that her most painful moments were when people who knew her would cross the street to avoid having to greet or talk to her. She understood that it was not a malicious act. She knew that they were at a loss of what to say or fearful that they might say the wrong thing. Nonetheless it hurt her to the core. She felt like a paraiah, alone and rejected. In those situations, one can simply say, " it is so good to see you" or "I've been thinking about you, "or "I've been praying for you" etc.—without prying or asking for medical report unless it's offered.

5. People cope differently, some are "attenders" and others are "distracters." The "attenders" get comfort from discussing and sharing their issues. The "distracters" prefer to talk about other things to get space and relief from their woes. We need to take our cue from the person and not impose our preference. Every human being copes and deals with pain differently. We know nothing of another person's life

and can never be in another person's shoes. Both externally and internally the worlds of two distinct individuals can never totally match.

6. Be specific in offers to help. Patty, recently widowed, shared that she immediately dismissed the offers of "call me when you need something." She felt they were totally unhelpful, if not insincere. A call asking her if today was a good time to take her shopping or to baby sit or to pick up something for her rang truer and more sincere.

7. Replacement strategies can be helpful. It is important to include those who have suffered losses into our lives, giving them space and letting them know they are welcome.

Joseph Stalin said "Education is a weapon whose effect depends on who holds it in his hands and at whom it is aimed".

The "repressive intolerance" within academia is coupled with a belief that human beings are social constructs. That is, our values, psychology, and sexuality—the very essence of our humanity—is the result of society's programming. It becomes necessary for the bad social construction to be demolished and replaced by proper programming. This is the goal of sensitivity or diversity training which often involves psychologically brutalising attendees.

The 90-minute "Blue Eyed" documents an experiment conducted by Jane Elliott, a $6,000 a day sensitivity trainer, in which a group of forty people are divided into blue eyes and brown eyed people. Thereafter, the former are psychologically brutalised and the latter are psychologically empowered as an object lesson in white racism. Elliott declares that this is what Newt Gingrich has been doing to minorities for years. The salvation of white people lies in the rooting out of subtle oppression such as the use of the name "Betty," which she serves to "infantilise women."

The success of Vasquez's self-stated devotion to eliminating "blame, ridicule, judgments, guilt, and shame" may be judged by some representative comments from attendees:

Brain: (Speaking about going to college amidst diverse groups)" I couldn't bridge both worlds if it comes to a choice I'm going with my people..."

Khanh (Asian): "White people ... you were taught to love yourself."

Judith: "I will not be less angry. I'm not here to tell you pretty things that it will be all right..."

Book Format Modules

Meaning of Modules: Modules are a type of planning in which the curriculums on the classroom instructional programmes are divided into small meaningful units called the 'modular units'. According to Allen and Bush, a module stands for a sub-part or sub-system of the curriculum or instructional programme.

Modules in Single Book Format: In a book form, a module usually include these aspects:

(1) Instructional objectives of the unit,

(2) Broad outlines of the content or learning experiences,

(3) Presentation schemes of the subject matter, and

(4) Evaluation pattern.

They are related to the class, size and length of the period.

Desirable features of a module

(1) It should focus on a distinct identifiable skill or set parts of skills.

(2) It should be fairly short.

(3) It should be essentially self teaching.

(4) It should be prepared in such a way that learning may not require the presence of the instructor.

(5) It should blend theory and practice, reading, reflecting and acting.

(6) It should involve the students in real or simulated situations.

Modular approach in teaching: (Packaging instructions)

Arranging instructional activities into a related set and organising the activities and the associated instructional materials into some sort of "package" has become a common practice. The general term for instructional packages in module. "A module is a self-contained set of learning experiences intended to facilitate the student's attainment of a stated set of objectives. Modules have different formals and organisation. In general, a module has the following five parts:

(1) Prospectus:- A statement of rationale to the learner.

(2) Statement of objectives:- A behavioural statement of the most important learning outcomes.

(3) Pre assessment:- A test to determine the learners need and readiness for the instructional activities.

(4) **Alternative enabling activities:-** A multipath set of learning activities designed to facilitate learning the behaviours described in the objectives.

(5) **Post assessment:-** A test to determine whether on not the learner can perform the behaviours described in the objectives.

Advantage of plasticising modular approach in teaching

(1) Attends to the diversity in background, readiness, requirements and personal objectives of learners.

(2) Makes more effective use of expensive human resources and provides cost-effective, individualised learning activities.

(3) Helps to overcome the demand for something more than role learning.

(4) Provides an increase in the amount, quality and availability of ERIC (Educational Research Information Centre) on learning and instruction.

(5) Helps to "keep up with the times" in the interest of institutional survival.

Module Approach

A module is an independent self-instructional material designed for a specific purpose which is a part of broader or comprehensive instructional system. Modules are a part of course contents which accounts for successful training programmes where each module consists of specific objectives. Approach: Approach is a path/method of technique which is followed to achieve the objective successfully. It may account for positive effect as well as negative effect. A systematic way/attempt which is followed so as to enhance the training. Programme successfully with some desired subject matter is useful for a teacher is known as modular approach. Individualisation of instruction is the need of the day. The learner's possess specific individual characteristic of learning and at their own pace. A moduler provides a learner the required material for learning at his own pace and self-efforts.

A module may be defined as a set of learning activities intended to facilitate the student's achievement of a set of objectives. A module usually is a sub-part or sub-system of the curriculum or instructional programme. However, as a subsystem (irrespective of it size) it is quite complete in itself with respect to providing desirable learning experience and self-instructional material to the learner. The whole curriculum can be divided into meaningful units called modular units or modules.

Components of a module

It includes:- (a) Objectives

(b) Contents covered

(c) Methodology of importing

(d) Evaluation.

Stages followed for a modular approach

(1) Overview of the topic with target group.

(2) Objectives in behavioural terms.

(3) Pre-testing and Post-testing.

(4) Reading materials.

(5) Re-testing.

(1) **Overview of the topic with target group:** It accounts for some innovative methodologies like:

(a) Inquiry method.

(b) Brainstorming method

(c) Simulation method.

(d) Role-playing method.

(2) **Objectives in behavioural terms:** It accounts for bringing some specific learning as according to the pre-estimated idea of objectives which are to achieve in terms of behavioural modification.

(3) **Pre-testing and Post–testing:** It pre-testing enables is to know the level of achievement at the very first stage and then the level of knowledge could be enhanced by follow up of some relevant method and thus achievement could be increased and could be estimated through the process of post-testing.

(4) **Reading materials:** It concentrates on the concept of course contents which includes:

(a) Encountering of problem.

(b) Gathering of information (verification)

(c) Experimentation

(d) Explanation

(e) Analysis of enquiry.

(5) **Re-testing:** This accounts for finalising of achievement of an individual which had led to an idea about his/her optimised extent of learning.

A sel- instructional module includes:

1. A set of instructional objectives of the module.
2. The broad lines of content or learning experiences.
3. The presentation of the subject matter in (a programmed form) an interactive style.
4. The evaluation system.

Structure of a module

1. Introduction for motivation and recalling the relevant knowledge.
2. Contents divided into subunits and presented.
3. Questions after each teaching point to check their progress.
4. A summary.
5. Unit end exercises.
6. Answers to questions to check their progress.

Educational implication of modular approach

(1) Concept can be learnt very specifically bit by bit.

(2) (Often) Frequent evaluation leads to better modification in the earlier process as followed.

(3) Objectives/Goals achieved are very definite in nature and are far from confusion or overlapping of ideas.

(4) Summarisation of the entire topic gives an overall icea of the subject matter very clearly.

(5) Sufficient materials can be gathered as and when needed for some special reference.

EXERCISES

1. What is Teaching strategy?
2. Briefly explain types of Teaching strategies.
3. What are the advantages of Brainstorming?
4. What is Sensitivity training?
5. How to spot Sensitivity training sessions?
6. What causes Insensitivity?
7. Briefly state modular approach in teaching.
8. What is Book Format Modules?

Chapter 5 Instructional Designs

Objectives

After completing this unit you will be able to:

- Explain Meaning and Characteristics of Instructional Designs
- State the Components of Instructional Designs
- Explain Objective-based Instructional Design
- Explain Skill-based Instruction Design
- Explain Competency-based Instructional Design
- Explain Learning Style-based Instructional Design
- Explain Model-based Instructional Design

INTRODUCTION

Concept

Instructional Designs provide the scientific basis for the instructional system. It develops the professional skill and efficiency of the teachers. The sequence of teaching acts or events that a teacher plans, organises and carries out in order to create a learning environment for the students is called the instructional design.

According to Glaser (1968) the functions of instructional designs are:

1. Analysis of instructional task for the structure of the content.
2. Analysis of learner's response in terms of objectives and levels of learning. Studying the entry behaviours of the students for providing appropriate stimuli for better performances.

3. Selecting teaching strategies, techniques and approaches for presenting the content so that the desired learning structures result.
4. Assessing the performance of students in order to find out if the objectives of learning have been realised.

An instructional design, is therefore, concerned with the structuring of the content to create a suitable learning environment, the selection of appropriate teaching strategies and methods and the assessment of performance level of students.

Instructional designs are the sums of teaching learning structures, teaching theories and structures of content. They are concerned with the application of modern skills and techniques for the requirement of education and training. This includes facilitation of learning by manipulation of media, methods and control of environment in so far as this reflects on learning.

Instructional designs have the following characteristics:

1. They emphasise structure of the task. Content is analysed for structure
2. They analyse learner's response in view of objectives and levels of learning.
3. They consider entering behaviour for providing new stimuli to have desired responses of the learner.
4. They involve the selection of appropriate teaching strategies, techniques and tactics for generating desired learning structures.
5. They employ the technique of motivation for leading the teaching.
6. They involve the construction of measuring instruments for evaluating the performance level of the learner.

An instructional design has different phases like:

1. Stimulating motivation.
2. Informing the learner, the objectives of learning.
3. Gaining and directing attention.
4. Activating recall.
5. Enhancing retention and transfer.
6. Providing learning guidance.
7. Eliciting performance.
8. Providing feedback.
9. Assessing performance.
10. Reviewing the process on the basis of assessment.

When a teacher designs his instructional hours he should be conscious of the need to motivate the students. This motivation should not only be at the beginning of the class but right through the class and the teacher should utilise all the opportunities which arise to motivate the students. Attention could be sought through motivation and the teacher should adopt several ways to maintain attention. Some of the other steps of an instructional design include listing the objectives of learning for the particular class or topic, enhancing retention of material learnt during the class by active questioning and providing feedback on the responses given by the students. These questions should not only aim at recalling but should invoke reflective thinking, receiving generalising and reasoning. Appropriate instructional aids and media should also be used for achieving better learning outcomes. The learning experience provided have to be assessed for replanning the instructional design.

Basic assumptions about instructional design

In planning and designing instruction, certain factors are fundamentals for proceeding with the designing task. They are:

1. The instruction can be oriented to the individual in spite of the fact that learners may be in large or small groups. An instructional design must aid at aiding individual learning.
2. Instructional designs may be both immediate and long–range. Design in the immediate sense relates to the preparation of the design a few hours before the instruction is given. The long–range approach takes time to plan and prepare not only the design of a particular topic but the whole courses itself or the entire instructional system itself. This approach involves more complex and varied designs. Such designs, developments are undertaken by individual teachers, team of teachers, curriculum planners and textbook writers.
3. Instructional design should be conducted by means of systems approach systems approach in instruction means planned, organised use of all available learning aids and instructional media, in order to achieve the desirable learning objectives by the most efficient way. It focuses on the learner and his performances first and then decisions are made regarding content, learning experiences, instructional media and strategies for realising the objectives.
4. Systematically designed instruction can greatly affect individual human development. A nurturing environment is not just adequate to develop an individual. Planning and directing are essential aspects of learning. An instructional design should ensure that no one is educationally disadvantaged.

5. Designed instruction must be based on knowledge of how human beings learn. Importance should not only be given to what the students should learn but also to how they should learn. An instructional design should take into account the learning conditions.

The Specification of Instructional Design

Design system may include

- **The designer:** The subject matter experts from content area. They may determine the objectives and the contents for the instructional system. They determine the sequence of presentation, methods and evaluation procedures. They convert the objectives and specifications into an actual instructional system.
- **The deliverer:** This includes the teachers and others in the instructional process like media projection experts.
- **The receiver:** The beneficiaries of the systems, which include the students or the learner.

This is an instructional system development project. Typically, the procedure is to identify specifications. The different stages in the procedure are:

1. Need assessment
2. Performance or task analysis: Need assessment leads to performance specifications and purposes. This stage helps in the identification of specific objectives. In this procedure various concepts, skills, and informational contents to be taught to the learners are identified

Task Analysis

Hierarchical information processing task analysis, this approach includes the following steps.

1. Arrange the operation and decision steps of procedure.
2. Sequence the steps in order in which they should be performed
3. Prepare a flow chart representation of the sequenced steps.
4. Validating the flow chart using several different initial inputs.

Designing for effective instruction:

Instruction is a human undertaking whose purpose is to help people to learn. Even though learning take place without instruction, instruction can help in accomplishing goal of learning. Instruction may or may not help in accomplishing the goal easily, but a well designed program of instruction helps in accomplishing the specific goal in prescribed time.

Instruction is a set of events that affect learners in such a way that learning is facilitated. Generally, an instruction is external to the learner like the talk of teacher or display of printed message. All those, which may have direct effect on learning of human being are included under instruction, not just the teacher talk. Teacher may play an important role in the arrangement of events. Teaching becomes only one form of instruction. Thus, the teacher should plan the instruction if it has to be effective. The teacher may not have time to plan his instructional technique minute to minute therefore, there is a need for structuring the instructional process and the design should be based on a theory and should be for the attainment of specific learning outcomes. Such a design may be a "model". Modeling is nothing but designing the instructional design.

A well designed instructional design should aim to the following:

1. It should help the learning of the individual
2. It should facilitate the learning of capabilities.
3. It should systematically be designed to affect individual human development.
4. It should follow a systematic approach so that learning is logical and goal-oriented.
5. It should be based on the knowledge of human beings learn, in other words, it should be based on valid learning theory. This means the model should take care of the learning conditions is designed to achieve the desired effect.

The presentation of learning situation during instruction is based on the following:

1. The principle of contiguity: The principle of contiguity states that the stimulus situation must be presented simultaneously with the desired response. Certain events are to be experienced contiguously by the learner in order for learning to occur, "objects once experienced together tend to become associated in the imagination, so that when any one of them is thought of, the others are likely to be thought of (James William, 1980, *Principles of Psychology* – Holt, Rinehart, and Winstone. New York)

2. Repetition: The principle of repetition states that the stimulus situation and its response need to be repeated or practiced for improved learning and retention (Gage, 1985).

3. Reinforcement: Learning of new act is strengthened when the occurrence of that act is followed by a satisfying state of affairs the learner should succeed in every act of learning to make him get satisfaction.

Trends in the field of instruction

Around 1950, educational research became a prevalent mode of enquiry with the quest for an "ideal" instructional design, there evolved a global perceptive that attempted to identify one instructional methods that was superior to all others. As a result researchers tended to investigate very general, gross variables and focused on comparison between major methods of instruction. Lecture was compared with discussion, Inductive methods were compared with detective methods, the discovery methods were compared with the expository approach, mediated instruction was compared with non mediated instruction.

It soon became apparent that the research results were contradictory, that any one of these methods could be designed and utilised in such a way has to be better than the alternative. So the field of "instruction" entered into a phase of analysis in which the methods of instruction work broken down into elementary components, called instructional strategy components such as rule example (rules and examples) method (Glaser, 1964) programmed instruction which is based on overt response reinforcement (Skinner, 1969).

These were the knowledge-based techniques. It was very difficult for instructions to match nature of knowledge with the competency to be developed, and also to 'mix and match' these piecemeal knowledge–based strategies to a holistic strategy. So various investigators have begun to usher the field of instruction into synthesis phase where the appropriate strategy components are combined into models of instruction.

The instructional models are supposed to be better than any other known combination for a specific situation. Hence, situations such as principle learning, problem solving provide the basis for prescribing instructional models. According the Reigeluth, even though a lot of progress is made in this direction much more work is to be done.

The components of instructional design at the lesson level

An instructional strategy component is a part of the instructional design. It is apart of the method of instruction, which influences the learning outcomes. So instruction has two major parts.

1. The instructional strategy component.
2. The learning situations which use the strategy component: The development of learning situations depends on the strategy to be used, which has to match the learning outcome. There are variations in these designs. The variations depend on the nature of the content and designed outcome.

There is a need to describe the general nature of instructional design and then go to the specific differences between the designs and the bases for variation.

1. The basic requirement of instructional designing is to perform the task of content analysis of instruction, this would definitely determine as 'What to teach'. This has already been discussed as top down analysis.
2. The second basic requirement is to decide how to teach. This is done after designing the overall structure and sequencing. (This requires a planned climb up analysis)

To do this there is a need to select a general design for the overall structure and sequence of the course.

The selection of general pattern of the design depends on the objectives and its domain. For example problem solving comes under the cognitive domain. Exhaustive information is available on this. This is the broadest level of instructional design. This has emerged out of sequencing the content in the form of task analysis. The ability to solve problem is kept in mind in task analysis. Therefore, this is referred to as macro-level instructional design, (Gagne and Brigs, 1979).

Ausubel's argument supplements this thinking. Sequencing in which learning occurs should influence the stability of cognitive structures. There by it should influence the long term retention and transfer. The process of further analyzing objectives and then sequencing them is repeated to match the internal condition of the learner. So that the external conditions are matched with internal conditions by creating proper learning situation. This process helps in deriving the performance objectives, these performance objectives are sequenced to make up a lesson.

Sequencing strategies

Poser (1976) suggests five types of organising principles, these five types may be combined to create instructional sequences. The five organising principles are:

1. **Word-related sequencing:** Development from past to present–future

2. **Concept-related sequencing:** Relationship between conceptual world and as it relates to real world.
3. **Inquiry-related sequences (inquiry modalities)**
4. **Learning-related sequences:** Based on the knowledge of psychology of learning.
5. **Sequencing-based on problem solving models:** This is based on the concept that problem solving is a type of learning.
6. **Utilization-related sequencing:** Problem solving based on utility.
7. **Bruner's Sequence:** It is a spiral curriculum. It prescribes that content be sequenced in tune with the learner's intellectual development. The sequence is to be built around the fundamental structure of the subject. The fundamental ideas or basic concepts are taught first and then the new concepts are developed with periodical recycling of the subject already taught. This produces a spiral and further learning with a greater degree of complexity is possible. Bruner does not give guidance as how to create the spiral sequence. Hence, it has not been easy to use this sequencing strategy.

(1) Ausubel's (1963) developed an instructional theory: which assumes that learner's "cognitive structures are hierarchically organized in terms of highly inclusive concepts under which are subsumed less inclusive sub concepts and informational data" (Ausubel, 1960, p-267). According to his theory the new stable cognitive are developed on detailed previous general knowledge.

(2) There is a general sequencing model suggested. It is called the elaboration approach. The elaboration theory starts instruction with special kind of overview containing the most fundamental ideas. Subsequent lessons add complexity or details to one part. Further subsequent lessons add greater complexity. It tries to relate the ideas already learnt to the most recent ideas. It believes in the following.

- Within lessons sequencing.
- Summarisers
- Synthesizers
- Analogies
- Cognitive strategy activators
- Learner control

The above points clearly speak about role of sequencing in the process of instruction. They are to be illustrated by the method teacher. The second component of a successful classroom instruction is about the strategy of teaching. The teacher or the school has to design the instructional strategy on each individual skill or piece of information. Such a design is called micro level strategy. It is method of working out details about examples to be given, mode of giving practice method of getting feedback about our success in instruction, memory devices used and attention getting devices. The decision should include which component is to be used, how much and what should each component be like. Robert Gagne, in America, was the first to use instructional strategy at the micro level. He identified nine events of instruction considered to be critical for effective instruction. These nine events are as follows:

1. Gaining attention.
2. Informing the learners of the objective.
3. Stimulating the recall of the prerequisite learning to activate the present learning.
4. Presenting the stimulus situation through stimulus materials.
5. Providing learning guidance.
6. Elicitation of performance.
7. Providing feedback about performance.
8. Assessing performance in order to evaluate learning.
9. Enhancing the retention and transfer.

The failure of many instructional programs has often been the result of an emphasis solely on content. The knowledge of instructional designing in actual practice is a technology, which reduces the load on teacher who always has a tough daily routine of handling variety of situations with students who have individual differences. Professional bodies of teachers and school management have to work in this direction to develop instructional designs suitable to their needs, based on the above ideas or any suitable idea which is suitable to their conditions.

Types of institutional designs

Instructional designs can be classified based on the teaching-learning process as related to teaching skills, Instructional objectives competencies or performance teaching strategies, teaching models and learning styles, thus they are classified into Objective-based Instruction Design, Instruction Design-Skill-based, Competing-based, Model-based, Learning style-based.

OBJECTIVE-BASED INSTRUCTIONAL DESIGN

Learning takes place when the students achieve what the teachers perceive as essentials to be achieved while a course or a unit of a course is taught in the classroom or outside it. In order to know if learning has actually taken place, the teachers should be clear about what they perceive as essential and how they expect the students to learn. In other words, the objectives of teaching must be specifically defined so that the teachers keep those as frame or reference to find out if learning has taken place and if so whether their teaching has been effective. It implies, therefore, that effectiveness of teaching is the outcome of adopting appropriate teaching techniques to help students achieve these objectives and of an appropriate evaluation to find out if learning has taken place. It follows that instructional objectives, teaching strategies and evaluation are the three salient features of effective teaching which indicates effective learning.

The teacher has to generate the instructional objectives from the curriculum of a particular course and use this as the guideline for his teaching. To the extent that these instructional objectives are made specific, observable and measurable and are adequately expressed in operational terms, the choice of appropriate teaching strategies and evaluation becomes easier.

The first step towards formulating objective-based instructional design is to have a clear concept of instructional objectives expressed in terms of student behavior. This can be done by analysing each of the general objectives into specific objectives. Several attempts have been made to analyse and of these, the efforts of Benjamin S. Bloom and his team have yielded practical results and indicated further possibilities.

Taxonomy of Educational Objectives

Bloom and his associates have classified and organised objectives collected by them into three categories as:

1. Cognitive Domain (Thinking process)
2. Affective Domain (Feeling)
3. Psychomotor Domain (Acting or Doing)

These three domains are considered in psychology as Cognition, Affection and Conation. Other than Bloom and his associates, notably

Krathwohl and Harrow have done considerable work in this area. In each domain, there are categories and subcategories, which are stated in terms of student behaviours. They are arranged according to hierarchy, indicating that higher objectives can be reached only if the previous lower ones are attained. Objectives relate to the subject of a course, a unit or a topic and it is possible to analyse the different syllabi to instructional objectives. Teachers need practice in spelling out the objectives in behavioural terms.

Cognitive Domain

The cognitive domain of educational objectives is concerned with the intellectual aspect of the mental process. This category consists of cognitive or thinking abilities. The six levels of learning in this domain are:

1. **Knowledge**— Knowledge is the lowest level of cognitive learning. The ability to recall or recognize specifics and universals, patterns and processes and ideas and facts are defined as knowledge level of learning.
2. **Comprehension**— Understanding what is being communicated and translating it through other means, interpreting specifics and extrapolation of the content communicated form this category.
3. **Application**— Application is the middle level objective of cognitive domain. Abstract information finds an application component when it is used in practical situations.
4. **Analysis**— Analysis leads to clarifying and organizing the different forms of communication and thereby expressing a relationship among them. This category develops the reasoning ability of the students.
5. **Synthesis**— In synthesis, all the elements are analyzed in such a way that they form a pattern or structure. By combining and organizing the elements a unique whole emerges. This objective enables to creative ability among students.
6. **Evaluation**—All the earlier categories are prerequisites of this category. The value of matter and method is assessed, quantitatively and qualitatively with reference to any given criteria.

A teacher identifies the teaching objectives in relation to three aspects, namely, needs of students, level of entering behaviour of students and the structure of the content or subject-matter. Based on these he states, the objectives in terms of the learning outcomes of the students. In the cognitive domain, he would be interested in developing percepts and concepts, factual information, generalization, judgment, problem solving and creativity. A college teacher should try to include all the objectives of learning and not 'knowledge' alone as it is done generally by many of the teachers at the tertiary level.

Affective Domain

Krathwohl (1964) and his associates analysed the affective domain educational objectives into five categories;

- Receiving (attending)
- Responding
- Valuing
- Organisation

* Characterisation of value or value complex.

Objectives that relate to feelings, emotion or a degree of acceptance or rejection come under the affective domain. The taxonomy deals with interests, attitudes, values, appreciation and adjustment. There is a marked difference between the objectives of the cognitive domain and affective domain that the correct response to a cognitive question is the same for all respondents whereas in affective domain the response depends on the social situation, the person being questioned, the type of question asked etc., The emphasis in the affective domain is on feelings rather than knowledge.

At the level of receiving, the learner is sensitised to the existence of certain stimuli so that he is willing to receive or attend to the stimuli. When the student is sufficiently motivated, he responds or actively attends and then finds pleasure or enjoys the activity. This level concerns with enjoyment of self-expression in music, arts and crafts. The category of valuing includes the worth of a thing or behaviour. Valuing results not by the desire to obey or comply but by the student's commitment to the underlying value that guides his behaviour. As the student successively internalises values, he starts building up his own value system. In this conceptualisation process, he organises his value system and synthesizes it into a value complex of higher order. The earlier four levels are the prerequisites of characterisation. The individual responds in relation to the values he has internalised and develops his own philosophy of integrated values and beliefs. As indicated earlier higher objectives can only be achieved if lower objectives have already been attained.

Psychomotor Domain

An analysis of psychomotor domain has been carried out by Elizabeth Simpson (1966), Dave (1968), Sumner (1971), Harrow (1972) and Simpson (1972).

Harrow's classification has six major categories:

- Reflex movements
- Basic fundamental movements
- Perceptual abilities
- Physical abilities
- Skilled movements
- Non-discursive communication

The psychomotor domain deals with abilities and sills which are physical in nature but activated by an inner mental process. These can be observed in the quality of human actions and doings. Any physical activity has to start with movements of some segment or other of the physical body. The reflex movements occur without our conscious effort and they can be segmental, intersegmental or super segmental. The basic fundamental movements of locomotion and non-locomotion come next in the hierarchy of psychomotor behavior, Perceptual abilities refer to the discrimination in the five-sense perceptions namely, seeing, touching, hearing, smelling and tasting and the co-ordination of the sense perceptions whenever necessary. Endurance, strength, flexibility and agility are the sub-abilities under physical abilities. Next in the hierarchy come the skilled movements, the simple and the complex adaptive skills. Non-discursive communication ability is the ability to communicate through expressive and interpretive movements. Psychomotor abilities are, thus, classified into six major objectives with sub–classification under each objective.

Methods of Writing Instructional Objectives

While there are various approaches to the writing of objectives in behavioural terms, Mager (1962), has indicated the following three criteria:

1. Identify the terminal behaviour or performance by specifying the type of behaviours that will show that the students have achieved the objectives.
2. Indicate the desired behaviour in terms of the conditions under which the behaviour or performance is expected.

3. Specify the minimum acceptable level of performance and the criteria for accepting.

Mager has pointed out that in writing each instructional objective, it is important to show the anticipated end performance of instruction, the conditions that would enable the learner to attain such a performance and the criteria for accepting the performance.

Associated action verbs used for stating specific instructional objectives

The college teacher has to be very specific in describing the behaviour that is expected of a student to demonstrate the mastery of the subject, topic or unit or a skill. Some of the associated action verbs are listed below to enable the college teacher to write the specific objectives.

Cognitive Domain

1. **Knowledge:** Define, state, list, name, describe, label, select, identify, match, reproduce.
2. **Comprehension:** Explain distinguish, convert, extend, formulate, represent, classify, rewrite, infer, justify, predict, give examples, contract.
3. **Application:** Change, compute, demonstrate, construct, solve, manipulate, select, assess, perform, show, use, operate.
4. **Analysis:** Analyse, separate, differentiate, contrast, relate, select, compare, sub-divide, resolve, breakdown, conclude.
5. **Synthesis:** Categorise, combine, restate, summaries, generalise, argue, relate, generate, plan, reconstruct, revise, rewrite, compose, create.
6. **Evaluation:** Judge, evaluate, criticise, justify, determine, derive, support, avoid, conclude, attack, relate.

Psychomotor Domain

1. **Reflex movements:** Respond, react, blink, withdraw, run.
2. **Basic fundamental movements:** Walk, run, move, skip, jump, handle, touch, take, hold, catch.
3. **Perceptual abilities:** Discriminate, find the differences, select, separate, group.
4. **Physical abilities:** Bear with, hold adapt, adopt, continue, carry.
5. **Skilled movements:** Manipulate, draw, dance, sing, play, speak.
6. **Non-discursive communication:** Gesture, use non-verbal cues, understands non-verbal messages

The student's development is concerned with all the three domains. In writing the lesson, it is good to indicate the teaching objectives in behavioural terms as the learning outcomes are complex and there is need to integrate the three domain's further following the teaching objectives, teaching material is prepared based on the objectives and the criterion test is developed on the same basis. The cycle of activities ensure an effective instructional design which is objective-based.

INSTRUCTIONAL DESIGN–SKILL-BASED

The activities that are performed by a teacher in the classroom may be classified as introducing, demonstrating, citing examples and exceptions, hypothesising, reporting, conjecturing, conforming, contrasting, explaining, elaborating and concluding. Some of these activities relate to skills of teaching as these activities lead to learning. A teacher involved in these activities will notice that certain specific activities emerge such as questioning the students, writing on the chalkboard, accepting students answers, rewarding by nodding, smiling and gesturing, illustrating, etc. These interrelated teaching acts which are observable, measurable and controlled and help in attaining the instructional objectives are called teaching skills. This analytical approach to teaching has assumed that teachers can be purposely trained to develop these teaching skills and use them judiciously in their teaching process.

A list of teaching skills developed at Stanford University, California is given below:

1. Stimulus variation
2. Set induction
3. Closure
4. Teacher silence and non-verbal cues
5. Reinforcing pupil participation
6. Fluency in questioning
7. Probing questions
8. Use of higher order questions
9. Divergent questions
10. Recognizing and attending behaviour
11. Illustrating

12. Lecturing (explaining)
13. Planned repetition
14. Completion of communication

Allen (1966) has indicated that' the identification of representative skills and the devotion of substantial time to these relatively narrow skills. will help teachers not only to become adept in the skills themselves but also to improve their original competence as well. Teachers can purposely and systematically practice one or two at a time and can improve their teaching skills, with peer group feedback or video feedback. The integration of teaching skills is expected to result out of continuous practice.

The explanation of the following teaching skills which will be useful for teachers is given below:

1. Set induction
2. Stimulus variation
3. Questioning
4. Explanation
5. Closure

Skill of Introducing a Topic (Set Induction)

The introduction to a lesson must be interesting so as to absorb the students in what follows. In spite of individual differences among students in regard to intelligence, attitude, personality, maturity level, etc., the teacher should plan the lesson in order to draw and sustain their interest. The components of this skill are :

1. Using previous knowledge
2. Using appropriate device

Introduction serves as a bridge between new knowledge and new topic and previously learnt knowledge. Appropriate devices used for an introduction are narrations, illustrations (charts, filmstrips, slides) questions, similarities and analogies. Care should be taken to see that there is a direct link between the new topic and previous knowledge. Relevant and logical statements are to be made. This part of the lesson would not take more than 5-7 minutes and the teacher adopts to use this skill in an apt manner.

Skill of Stimulus Variation

An important skill is trying to hold the attention of the class. Preparations made by the teacher will be futile if the students are not attentive. This skill involves using various attention producing behaviour patterns in order to sustain the interest and attention of the students. The following are the components of stimulus variation.

1. Purposeful movements: Teachers movements are planned and purposeful such as moving towards the chalkboard to write a new word or draw a diagram, to go near a student to observe his work, move to the table to demonstrate an experiment, etc. Unnecessary movements in strolling across the length of the room or walking towards the students with no specific purpose should be avoided.

2. Meaningful gestures: Making use of hand movements and facial expressions are permitted in classrooms these days. Some of theses non-verbal communication patterns are very effective if used properly at the appropriate time and place.

3. Change in speech patterns: The intensity and pitch of voice and the speed of speech can be modulated to express different types of feelings and emotions. This will also avoid boredom in the classroom.

4. Change in interaction styles: Changing the interaction styles of the teacher is helpful to sustain interest. The change can be from teacher and group interaction as in the case of a lecture class to teacher-student interaction (questioning) or student-student interaction (discussion).

5. Change in the sense channels: The teacher need not keep to the sense of hearing (perhaps seeing) alone. A manual activity can be introduced or illustrations, pictures, charts may be shown to bring a change in students reception of channel of sense–from audio to oral-visual or visual.

6. Change in postures: Teacher can change his posture from standing to sitting or sitting to standing, bending, leaning forward to emphasise an important idea. However, dramatisation should be avoided as much as possible.

Skill of Questioning

Feedback from students is best achieved by questioning. Questioning helps the teacher to understand how far the teaching has been helpful to his students. The teacher can evaluate the effectiveness of his teaching then and there on the basis of the feedback of student's answers to the questions asked. This questioning method also helps the students to know how far they have been able to grasp the idea.

Questions are generally of three types: (1) Lower order, (2) Middle order, (3) Higher order and each type has its own functions as well as merits. However, for students, higher order questions will be profitable, as these could result in the development of the most desirable aspects of the cognitive domain.

Lower order questions are those questions which merely test the ability to recall.

Middle order questions test the grasp of the subject and the ability to apply it. Questions which require interpretations and application of ideas, citation of examples, extrapolation, procedural sequence etc., come under middle order questions and these too can be encouraged in classes.

Higher order questions can develop higher mental abilities like analysis, synthesis, evaluation and creativity and increase critical awareness. These questions generally take the shape of 'why' or 'how'. The answers given by the students may be (1) correct, (2) completely wrong. (3) one part correctly answered, (4) partially right or partially wrong.

The teachers may use the techniques of prompting, probing and redirecting and thus, follow up the questions.

Prompting

Questions can be broken up into parts where the initial question is difficult to answer. Further clues or hints may be given for the students to complete.

Probing

When the initial response by the student is incomplete or partially correct, questions requiring the students to clarify elaborate or explain his initial answer may be asked.

A student may further be questioned on a correct answer for relating it to another similar situation and thus help the student to view the response in a broader perspective. The student may be helped in his reasoning by asking 'how' and 'why', when the initial question is answered correctly.

Redirecting

A discussion can be stimulated among the students by asking other students to answer the same question or addressing it to the class in general. Redirecting technique increases student's participation. As we have seen different types of questions are asked to make the students exercise their power or recall and recognition, exercise their reasoning ability, reflect over things and ideas, compare and contrast things or ideas and initiate the students to a discussion.

Skill of Explanation

The skill of explanation is one of the common skills adopted by many college teachers without understanding its full scope and effect on the learners. To explain is to make ideas, concepts, events and actions clear. It can also relate ideas, events and principles. However, in reality giving explanations appears to be more difficult than making factual statements or reports. When a teacher is using the skill of explanation, he uses the verb, "how" and "why" in relation to a concept or event or condition. Phrases such as ' as a result' , 'therefore', 'in order to 'and 'through' are also used to indicate the links. These key verbs and phrases help in directing the process of explanation. There are a few factors that contribute to the effectiveness of the skill of explanation and these are continuity, simplicity and explicitness.

Continuity

Continuity has two components, sequence and fluency. A lesson should indicate the sequence of the ideas explained. Diversions from the main theme should be minimal. If diversions are necessary, as they happen due to pupil participation, there should be pointed as diversions. However, the relevance to the main theme should be understood by the students. Discontinuity in a theme can be noticed when a teacher changes the topic or his line of argument without indicating the connection between what he has been saying to what he has now started to say.

Fluency

Fluency of explanation depends on the mastery of the subject matter, ability to communicate the ideas coherently and self-confidence to manage the class. In addition, the important factor is advance planning of the discourse. Students understand an explanation when the teacher uses easily intelligible grammatical sentences. Lack of fluency is indicated by the number of times a teacher reframes the sentences and sometimes leaves the sentences unfinished.

Simplicity

Some teachers have the pleasure of making their explanations sound very complex. Perhaps this is due to the fact that too much of information is given in one and the same sentence. Sentences should be short. Complex relationship can be explained through the aid of diagrams, charts, models, etc.

The vocabulary of the teacher must be within the reach of the students. Use of specialist terms without clarity is not of much help in explanation. Simple language within the student's normal vocabulary leads to effective communication. Special attention may be given to explain specialist terms when introduced.

Explicitness

In addition to the components of explanation skills, continuity, simplicity and explicitness, a clear explanation depends on the identification of the aspects to be related (objects, events and processes) and identification of the relationship among the components. Theses two process are of vital importance to explaining skill and the teacher has to practice this purposefully. The teacher's failure to do this is a primary cause of confused presentation.

An appraisal guide can be prepared to assess the use of explanation skill, with the following positive and negative factors.

Positive

Use of explaining links

Objects and relations between them identified

Use of visual techniques for explanation

Continuity of the theme

Negative

Unexplained vocabulary

Vague words or sentences

Unnecessary technical terms

Grammatically over complex sentences

Questions presented to the learners without giving a chance to answer

Unfinished sentences

A teacher can use audio recording to record his teaching lessons and play it back to assess his own performance or get the help of his colleagues to evaluate his performance.

Skill of Closure

The skills, set induction and closure complement each other. Just as there is need to introduce the lesson, so too attention must be given to the concluding part of the lesson. Closure is related to the end part of a lesson or end of a specific learning sequence. The components of the skill consist of proper timing of the various learning activities in the classroom in order to allot at least five minutes for this, reviewing the key points of a lesson and indicating the material so far dealt with and what is expected for the next lesson. Closure skill could also be demonstrated by ending a discussion or laboratory exercise by summarising the major aspects covered during a lesson. The skill is a very simple skill, easy to follow but invariably teachers don't plan for it and are caught up with the bell being rung and students getting ready to leave or prepare for the next lesson. A proper closure to lesson not only gives a clarity to the extent of content covered, both to the teacher and the learner but also a review of the key points of the lesson and what to look for in the next lesson

Additional skill – Discipline wise

Teachers could identify certain special skills needed and used by teachers of a particular discipline. Some of the special skills identified by teachers for science subjects are skill of demonstration, skill of manipulating certain special apparatus and equipment and skill of problem solving. For the teaching of languages, skill of reading, writing and listening are required. The disciplines of mathematics and commerce would specially involve the use of the skill of reading and interpreting statistical data. The skill of observation and evaluation would be related to many if not all the disciplines. It depends on the ingenuity of the teacher to identify the particular skill or skills needed for their discipline and become adept in using those skills.

Linking the various skills

With the knowledge of the various skills and their components the teacher can purposely practice using each skill or combination of two skills in a few of his lessons so that he becomes efficient in these skills. It is advisable to have self and/or peer group feedback. After gaining experience in the use of skills, individually or in combination of two or three, the teacher should make an attempt to use all of them in a single lesson, as per the needs. The developed skills have to be orchestrated, the right skill at the right time in the right proportion. The skill used in a particular context of the lesson should be relevant, timely and appropriate; otherwise there will be only a mixture of skills and not effective blending. There is need to have opportunities to practice the skill in a link-lessons (linking of the different skills in a lesson) and to get evaluative feedback to improve the linking of skills, a judicious use of teaching skills enhances teaching effectiveness and efficiency. The instructional design that involves the use of teaching skills is generally termed as skill-based approach is feasible or not every teacher should be aware of the teaching skills and the need to develop and improve these for effective teaching.

INSTRUCTIONAL DESIGN – COMPETENCY–BASED

Competency-based education, also known as performance-based education is a new approach to teaching, having as its core, the ideas of accountability and competencies. With regard to accountability it is argued that teachers should be held 'accountable' for their products. This accountability is accomplished by breaking teaching into discrete competencies or behaviors which can be stated as objectives. Mastery of these competencies is then possible (Unwin and McAleese, 1978).

Competency-based education rests upon a few assumptions which are generally shared by educationists they are:

1. Learning takes place through changes in the behaviors of learners and that teaching aims at facilitating these changes.
2. Individuals achieve similar objectives but at different rates.
3. Teachers should be accountable for the learning that takes place in their students.
4. Continuous evaluation of teaching is used as a feedback for revising the instructional programme and this in turn promotes effective teaching.
5. The objectives of any educational programme bears close relationship to the educational goal.
6. Systems approach can be applied to education, especially to instructional planning and designing.

In competency-based education competencies are spelled out so that it is possible to assess student learning through direct observation of student behaviour. The student knows in advance the extent and level of competencies to be mastered by him. They are measured in the form of specified learner behaviors. In order to facilitate this, performance goals are specified and agreed to in great detail much in advance of instruction. The teacher is held accountable, not for his students 'obtaining a passing grade' but for attaining a given level of competency in performing the essential tasks of learning. Student's progress rate depends on demonstrated competencies. The emphasis is laid on exit and not on entrance requirements. Further the focus is being on acquisition of specific competencies by all the students. Time becomes variable and depending on the needs and capabilities of the learner, he is allowed to attain the competencies at his own rate and space.

Elam (1971), explains five basic features of competency-based programme

1. Competencies to be demonstrated by the students are derived from explicit conceptions of teacher roles and are publically stated in such a manner that students learned behaviours are related to specified competencies.

2. Criteria to be employed in assessing competencies are stated in terms of expected levels of mastery under specified conditions.

3. Assessment of competency depends on student performance as the primary source of evidence and strives for objectivity.

4. Students rate of progress is determined by demonstrated competencies rather than time or course completion.

5. Instructional programme is intended to facilitate the development of specified competencies.

Competency-based education is, therefore, unique in the sense that it focuses on the student's acquisition of pre-specified, agreed upon competencies and demonstration of these specified competencies through objective assessment. Learning or instructional objectives are made explicit and the achievement of these objectives is observed in the modification of learner behaviour. Minimum levels of achievement of these objectives are the established criteria of success.

Instruction is presented in models, a module being a set of learning activities with objectives, pre-requirements, pre-assessment, instructional activities, post assessment and remediation. Modularisation helps in self-pacing, individualisation, and independent study. The use of modules allows a much greater variety of experience than standard courses and provides a far better basis for personalised construction. Many competency-based education programmes make use of self-instructional modules.

Criterion-referenced testing is an integral part of competency-based teacher education. Criterion-referenced tests are those kinds of tests that indicate whether the learner has achieved the goal specified for the learning tasks. They do not make a reference in comparison to the performance of other learners. It is considered that the criterion-referenced tests are more sensitive than norm-referenced tests for the purposes of detecting instructional efforts. They can provide the only relevant information on students learning excellence or deficiency.

Competency-based education is unique in the sense that it shifts that emphasis from testing the memory to the demonstration of required competencies and thereby emphasises outputs, they are not teacher–oriented but student–oriented. The principal, staff member of a concerned discipline at a particular level, undergraduate or post graduate should evolve the academic scheme. The first step is the preparation of instructional modules suited to the level of a target group. Time is not a factor but the possibility of attaining the competencies specified by the working team, by all students at that level is more important. The prepared modules can be tried out with a small group of students. Implementation of the modules with supporting materials such as books, booklets, and cassettes, slides and film strips, if necessary, will form the second stage. Students will not be permitted to proceed to the next unit of a module unless they master the competencies in that unit. A criterion-referenced test based on the pre-specified competencies should be conducted to ascertain the proficiency of the students. If the performance of the student is satisfactory they are allowed to proceed to the next lesson unit. When it is found that some of the students are lagging behind in mastering the competencies, time may be given for attaining the competencies. In some cases a different set of instructional package is needed as students have different patterns of learning and communicating. In case the instructional objectives or the competencies based on them are found to be unsuitable for that particular group the whole programme needs recasting. There may be non-academic reasons such as emotional and personal problems of the students that could hinder the mastery of the competencies. The different competencies students will acquire can be more accurately reflected by a well-defined criterion-referenced test in contrast to its counterpart, the norm-referenced tests.

The difficulties experienced by such students can be identified and referred to a teacher or some other qualified person for guidance and counseling. Since the personal and academic problems are intertwined and mutually interacting, cooperation between the class teacher and the counselor when the help of such a person is requisitioned, is essential for redressing the problems the student faces.

Realising the vital role that the competency-based education could play in cognitive development of school students, teachers could make a modest beginning in preparing competency-based modules on specific topics and try them out on small groups. The instructional design, based on competency-based education is yet another approach to efficient learning.

INSTRUCTIONAL DESIGN–MODEL-BASED

Teaching involves a variety of activities aimed at changing the student's behaviour. In turn, students with their multi-dimensional personalities, have different learning styles. The teachers, therefore, create the needed environment for the full development of the learner potentials; they adopt different teaching strategies to teach large groups, small groups or individuals. These strategies are based on certain philosophical, psychological and sociological considerations. However, these theories are not put into practice in many situations. Joyce and Weil (1985), have developed the concept of models of teaching. A model of teaching according to them is a plan or pattern that can be used to shape curriculum (long-term courses of study), to design instructional materials and to give instruction in the classroom and other settings. The core of the teaching model is that the learning outcomes can be classified into distinctive categories and each objective can be achieved by creating specific situations.

From a large list of models that are available, Joyce and Weil have selected 22, which are grouped into four families of models:

- Information-processing Models,
- Personal Models,
- Social Interaction Models, and
- Behaviour Models.

Information-processing Models

Information-processing models of teaching provide opportunities to the students for the development of their cognitive skills in terms of information-processing capability. Information process relates to the ways people handle stimuli from the environment, organise data, sense problems, generate concepts and solutions to problems and employ verbal and non-verbal symbols. Some of these modules are related to concept attainment and concept formation (Bruner, Goodnow and Austin), inductive approach (Taba), meaningful verbal learning theory (Ausubel), and cognitive development (Piaget) Emphasis is being given in some models to problem solving abilities resulting in productive thinking and in others general intellectual abilities. This family of models stresses social relationship and the development of an integrated, functioning self.

Personal Models

Personal growth models aim at the development of the self. They emphasise the processes by which individuals construct and organise their unique reality. Non-directive techniques and synectics methods are followed in this model. Roger's non-directive method assumes that by developing self-awareness, understanding autonomy and self-concept, a student can handle his own life situations in a constructive way. The teacher respects this capacity of the student and enables him to formulate solutions to his identified problems. Creative methods aim at personal development of creativity and creative problem solving. Personal models focus on helping students to view themselves in relation to their environment and become capable persons who can have rich interpersonal relationships.

Social Interaction Models

Social interaction models give priority to democratic processes in learning, the improvement of the ability of the students to relate to others and to work productively in society. Group methods come under this family of models. In the group-learning situations, the roles of the teacher changes to guiding, leading and giving help only when needed or required. In some cases the presence of the teacher may not be necessary when he has helped the group in the preparation of the concerned group activity. Some of these methods are buzz groups, brain storming, case discussion, syndicate group, tutorials, seminars, symposia, and discussion forums.

Behaviour Models

The fourth type of models, behaviour modification model, uses mainly reinforcement theory to sequence learning tasks and shaping behaviour. Operant conditioning (Skinner, 1951) is the core of the behaviour modification theories. The models focus on the modification of the external behaviour of the learners and describe the changes in relation to the visible behaviour rather than the unobservable behaviour. More than any other type of models, behaviour models have been applied in education, specifically in training, interpersonal relationships and in classroom management, for both individuals and groups they deal with situations in which the teacher is in control of the learning situation and also the instructional process where the learner is in control.

The families of models explained so far are not mutually exclusive. Each is based on some theory and represents a distinctive approach to teaching. There is a need for teachers to understand the techniques of the models, learn to make use of them in their teaching. Further, a teacher can develop his own teaching model which will be based on some of the principles and techniques adopted in the repertory of models and the needs of his learners.

INSTRUCTIONAL DESIGN—LEARNING STYLE-BASED

Of recent origin are the research studies on the styles of learning adopted by the learners. Students use different approaches when faced with learning tasks and problems. The way in which the students approach the learning tasks and the behaviour in learning situations determine their learning style. Rosenberg (1968), defines learning style as referring to 'an individual's characteristic pattern of behaviour when confronted with a problem. It is pointed out that the learning style of an individual has relation to factors such as prior learning experiences, openness to intrapersonal and extra personal information, physical facilities, and learning environment.

On the basis of the work of researches on learning, Rosenberg has arrived at four general learning-patterns which are rigid-inhibited style, undisciplined style, acceptance-anxious style and creative style. It should be noted that when categorizing an individual as belonging to a given learning style because he exhibits the characteristic of that style, he should be considered first and foremost as an individual person rather than a member of a particular category.

Learners with a rigid–inhibited style of learning require constant supervision as they get confused easily. They tend to give unrelated response to questions put forward. Changes in the class routine easily upset them and they also exhibit signs of nervousness. They depend on the support given to them by the teachers. The behaviour of the rigid-inhibited learner is, therefore, a problem to himself and his teacher. The 'undisciplined' learner exhibits characteristics such as refusal to obey commands, showing disrespect to teachers, deceiving, stealing, bullying, etc. Such learners invariably leave their learning task unfinished due to lack of tolerance. They concentrate on what gives them pleasure at the moment.

The learner under the category of acceptance – anxious cannot endure the thought of being wrong and therefore he tends to worry excessively about pleasing others. His desire for approval is so strong that it prevents him from working effectively his learning problem. This type of learners suffers greatly from tension and frustration.

The fourth type of learning style according to Rosenberg is creative style. Learners of creative style are self-confident, and able to evaluate their own performance with objectivity. They are prepared to learn from their mistakes and show divergent thinking ability. Anxiety stimulates their functioning, especially during the learning process rather than impair it. A creative learner continues with the learning task until he completes it, which gives him satisfaction. He performs well on a variety of tasks. Being a creative learner, he thinks independently and divergently and, therefore, also prefers to work independently.

There are several other approaches to classifications of learning styles. Depending on how a person looks at the whole problem. Kagan (1965), discuss about impulsive-reflective dimensions of learning style. Teachers tend to group students as obedient or disobedient, timid or outgoing, bright or dull rather than as reflective or impulsive. A reflective individual may be categorised as a dull student and impulsive quick individual as bright. Both electiveness and impulsiveness are related to the individual's conceptual thinking. Impulsiveness may lead to meeting with difficulties such as proceeding to work out a problem without understanding it, starting an experiment without following the instructions properly. Completing a reading passage without understanding the major concepts, etc. Reflectiveness is indicated in trying to comprehend material that has a variety of complex concepts in a passage above the level of students or in going over remedial work. Impulsivity can result in developing anxiety and consequently being punished and ridiculed by teachers and classmates, especially when it is associated with the speed of response.

There are also learning styles characterised as dependent-independent, co-operative-non co-operative, anxiety free-anxiety prone, competitive-noncompetitive; study habits–oriented–trial and error attempts, etc. Teachers can identify their own students learning styles by probing into their learning patterns some of which can be indicated indirectly in the classroom through teacher-student interactions in the valuation of academic performances and in the specific behaviour patterns. From the above classifications, the teachers surmise first, the existence of different styles of learning adopted by students and secondly, the effect of these styles on the learning process. Consequently, the instructional design could be based on learning styles, where the planning, preparation and conduct of a lesson emphasises learning styles of the students. The teacher's design of instruction should provide opportunities to the students who use different learning patterns. Teachers should also make an attempt to reduce the factors that do not encourage good learning styles such as anxiety, frustration and emotional instability, dependence on teachers and parents, rote memory and convergent thinking.

Combination of teaching strategies and instructional designs

Teaching strategies aim at establishing relationship between teaching inputs and learning outcomes, mainly in terms of realising the learning outcomes. Teaching strategies include teaching methods, approaches and techniques such as lecture method, tutorial approach, case study technique, demonstration method, team-teaching approach, programmed instruction, etc. In planning an instructional design, the teacher selects a particular essential factor to base his design such as objectives, skills, competencies, models or learning styles. In doing so, he focuses attention to the type of design he is going to prepare. The teaching strategies used to elaborate the content or subject-matter of that unit or topic.

Teaching strategies when designed with clearly spelt-out objectives and effective means of achieving them with inbuilt evaluation techniques is known as educational technology. Application of technology will ensure the achievement of objectives with the minimum effort and time required. When teaching results in effective learning of all the students taught, then any strategy that is applied to achieve this can be called educational technology. Educational technology is not deterministic, in the sense that if 'x' is done, 'y' will certainly happen. It only says that the probability of 'y' happening is very high if 'x' is done. The teaching strategies suggested have the high probability of effecting effective learning in students. Practising teachers may have to bring about some modifications, minor changes and adapt them to further increase the probability of their success in helping students learn more and better, and that is what educational technology, and for that reason, any technology is for.

EXERCISES

1. Briefly explain Meaning and Characteristics of Instructional Designs.
2. State the Components of Instructional Designs.
3. Explain Objective-based Instructional Design.
4. Explain Skill-based Instructional Design.
5. Explain Competency-based Instructional Design.
6. Explain Learning Style-based Instructional Design.
7. Explain Model-based Instructional Design.

Chapter 6

Models of Teaching

Objectives

After completing this unit, you will be able to:

- Explain Meaning, Nature and Features of Models of Teaching
- List out Elements of a Model
- State Characteristics of a Model of Teaching
- List out Information Processing Family of Models
- Explain Social-interaction Family of Models
- Mention the Personal Family of Models
- Explain Concept Attainment Model
- State Laboratory training Model
- How to Use Models Effectively in a Classroom

INTRODUCTION

The term 'model' generally means the representation of an overall view/idea about one particular concept that which may account in quantitative and qualitative aspect. Even the great philosopher Socrates used his own model known as "Dialect Model" (Question-Answer type).

Models of teaching have been developed to help a teacher to improve his capacity to reach more children and create a richer and more attempts to create efficient systems by sequencing learning activities and shaping behaviour by manipulating reinforcement. This instructional model is purely psychological model which has been used in most of the teaching strategies developed in the last two decades.

According to Joyce Bruce and Marsha Weil (1972), "Models of teaching are instructional designs that describe the process of specifying and producing particular environmental situations which causes the students to interact in such a way that specific change occurs in their behaviour."

NOTE

(1) The main aspect of Models of Teaching is that learning outcomes can be classified into distinct categories and each objective may be achieved by generating specific situation.

(2) Models of teaching can be applied to all sorts of content like Mathematics, Science, Social problems, Arts etc.

Principles of teaching are not static tenets but are dynamically interactive with social and cognitive purpose, with the learning theory underlying procedures, with available support technology, and with the personal and intellectual characteristics of learning groups. The teacher has a wide range of options to adopt and adapt to his unique situation. There exists a delightful and vigorous array of approaches to teaching that can be used to transform the world of schools if we employ them.

The strength in education resides in the intelligent use of the powerful variety of approaches matching them to different goals and adapting them to the students. Competence in teaching is the capacity to reach out to differing children and to create a rich and multidimensional environment for them. Curriculum planners need to design learning centers and curricula that offer a variety of educational alternatives. Instructional materials developers needs to create more interesting and effective books, films, and other learning sources. Most important, our society needs to develop new educational forms and educational opportunities. Models of teaching are one basis for the repertoire (needs) of alternative approaches that teachers, curriculum makers and designers of materials can use to help diverse learners reach a variety of goals.

"A Model of teaching in a plan or pattern that can be used to shape curriculums (long-term courses of studies), to design instructional materials, and to guide instruction in the classroom and other settings"

As we learn about the models and their uses, we find that the task of selecting appropriate modes is complex. The forms of "good" teaching are numerous depending on our purposes. Teaching is a process by which teacher students create a shared environment including sets of values and beliefs which in turn colour their view of reality. The "models" of teaching that we choose say about these realities of classroom and the kind of life-views likely to be generated when teacher and learner work together. Hence, the educators have sought for the perfect model – the approach to teaching that will solve all educational problems that will help every student learn everything in every way.

But there is no perfect model. No model of teaching is designed to accomplish all types of learning. Bruce Joyce and Marsha Weil assume that there are many kinds of learning, requiring different methods of instruction. They also assume that it comes with different learning styles, need different approaches if they have to become a productive and effective learner. Hence, we should not limit our methods to any single model, however attractive it may seem. No single approach succeeds with all students. So, instead of searching for a single right way we have to concentrate on the rich variety of models of teaching that our heritage has given. Our task is to develop an environment in which the student is taught in the variety of ways that facilitate his development.

B.Joyce and Marsha Weil conducted a long search for useful model of teaching and found them in abundance. Some of them have been invented by classroom practitioners. Some are the result of research in psychology and training. Many of the models came from therapists and many from philosophers. Many educational models have been developed by people engaged in different kinds of activity. Models are based on practice, empirical work theories, hunches, and on speculation about the meanings of theories and research done by others. Some are easy to use while others are complex and difficult to master. Few have broad purposes while some are useful for particular goals only.

From an enormous list of models B. Joyce and Marsha Weil have selected around 25 and grouped them into four families that represent distinct orientation toward people and how they learn.

Syntax– As the heart of a model

Syntax is one such element within a model of teaching which mainly accounts for the concept of grammatical rules and regulations based on specific conditions and criterion bounded with some phases which could be analyzed very systematically for proper accumulation of knowledge.

Syntax– As a heart of model – this statement satisfactorily holds goods as:

(1) Syntax is bounded with different stages/phases which are logically or sequentially arranged.

(2) Syntax gives the teacher an idea as to what way one has to follow for making use of the model.

(3) Syntax gives the teacher an idea of when a particular model could be used in relation to which particular subject and content.

(4) Syntax disciplines the work for making it to be processed very systematically.

(5) Syntax controls and co-ordinates the entire functioning of model very clearly.

(6) Syntax enables the teacher to know about the ideas of strategies/tactics/methods that are to be made use of in undertaking a specific model.

Nature of models of teaching

The nature of models of teaching are accountable for the following aspects:

(1) Models of teaching account for a systematic process with a scientific procedure to modify the behaviour of learners.

(2) Models of teaching must be applicable to the content of area as concerned and must also lead for a proper environmental situation of pleasing and favouring conditions of optimisive learning.

(3) Models of teaching should also enrich the interaction between the teacher and learner.

(4) Models of teaching should also include teaching strategies, styles, techniques and tactics of teaching with some relevant skills.

(5) Models of teaching should be largely accountable for the improvement of the performance of individual and thus, must also lead for allround development of personality of an individual.

Salient features of models of teaching

Most models of teaching serve as simplifying metaphors to reduce the fantastic complexity of human interaction as it occurs in the classroom. A model provides the answer to four questions.

- What do you want to know? Scope of the model
- How will you describe what you see? Description – general or specific.
- How often will you look?
- How many variables will you use at the same time?

The answer to the first question sets the scope of the model. Is everything in the classroom to be explained, or just a few things?

The second answer indicates whether your description will be general or specific, broad or detailed.

The third answer indicates the frequency of observation.

The fourth is little difficult. The human mind can judge with half a dozen variables at once.

There has to be a balance between scope, specificity and the number of variables. If the scope is modest, and the variables specific enough to be recognised, then a C-R teacher may be able to use them

Uses of models of teaching

(1) Models of teaching enhance all basic concepts of teaching and learning.

(2) Models of teaching are also useful for achieving the aims and objectives of teaching successfully.

(3) Models of teaching are very useful as they account with good member of experiences related to both teaching and learning aspects.

(4) Models of learning are useful for creating a very favourable environment for their real behavioural outcome of learners.

(5) Models of teaching are very useful for sequential, systematic, accurate and specific accumulation of intellectual knowledge.

ASSUMPTIONS OF MODELS OF TEACHING

Models of teaching have been evolved on the following assumption:

1. The first assumption underlying all models of teaching is that teaching is the creation of appropriate environment. There are various component parts of the teaching environment which are interdependent.
2. The second assumption is that content, skill, instructional roles, social relationships, types of activities, physical facilities and their use, all form an environment system whose parts interact with each other to constrain the behaviour of all participants, teachers as well as students.
3. The third assumption is that different combinations of these elements create different types of environments and elicit different outcomes.
4. The fourth and the last assumption is that models of teaching create environment. They provide rough specification for environment in the classroom teaching-learning process.

ELEMENTS OF A MODEL

A model has the following elements:

1. A focus
2. A syntax
3. A social system
4. A support system.

1. Focus: A focus of a system refers to the frame of reference around which the model is developed. It is the main thesis which determines combinations and relationship of various processes, conditions and factors built into the model. Objectives of teaching and aspects of the environment, generally, constitute the focus of the models. What is aimed to be achieved is found to be the focus of most of the models. Focus is the central aspect of a teaching model.

2. Syntax: The second element, syntax or phasing of the model, refers to the description of the model in action, i.e., the kind of activities which are organised as well-defined stages of the whole programme typify the educational environment belonging to each model. It is the sequence of steps involved in the organisation of the complete programme of teaching.

3. Social system: The third element is the social system which refers to two elements students and teacher roles, particularly, hierarchical relationship or authority relationships, and norms or the students behaviour which is rewarded. Social system is an important element of every model. Specific learning's are very much controlled by the kinds of relationship that are structured during the process of teaching. Models of teaching prescribe system for teaching of attitudes, skills and understandings etc.

4. Support system: The last and the most important aspect of a model is the support system which means to provide facilities to teacher and the students to successfully implement the strategy of teaching. For example, if we want to implement individualisation, we have to provide a number of audio-visual aids, teaching machines, programmed text etc., to cater to the needs of individual learner.

In the following table we have classified models of teaching on the basis of their sources. It will not be possible to describe all the models so we will follow sample approach. The following models have been selected for detailed treatment.

S. No.	Source 1	Model
1	Social interaction	Group investigation model
2	Social interaction	Social inquiry model.
3	Information processing	Inductive teaching model.
4	Information processing	Concept attainment model.
5	Information processing	Developmental model.
6	Information processing	Advance organizer model.
7	Person	Non-directive teaching model.
8	Person	Classroom meeting model.
9	Behaviour modification.	Operant conditioning model.

A model of teaching has been defined in various ways by research workers who worked in the field of teaching.

One of the most comprehensive definition runs as, "Model of teaching can be defined as an instructional design which describes the process of specifying and producing particular environmental situations which cause the students to interact in such a way that a specific change occurs in their behaviour"

CHARACTERISTICS OF A MODEL OF TEACHING

All good models of teaching have some common identifiable characteristics which are described as follows:

1. **Scientific procedure:** A model of teaching is not a haphazard combination of facts but on the other hand it is a systematic procedure to modify the behaviour of learners. They are based on certain assumptions.
2. **Specification of learning outcome:** All models of teaching specify the learning outcomes in detail on observable student's performance. What the student will perform, after completing an instructional sequence, is specified in detail.
3. **Specification of environment:** This means that every model of teaching specifies in definite terms the environment conditions under which a student's response should be observed.
4. **Criterion of performance:** A model specifies the criteria of acceptable performance which is expected from the students. The model of

teaching delineates the behavioural outcomes which the learner would demonstrate after completing specific instructional sequences.

5. **Specification of operations:** All models of teaching specify mechanisms that provide for students reaction and interaction with the environment.

FUNCTION OF A MODEL OF TEACHING

The basic question which may be asked by a reader here, is why should we develop a model of teaching and what are its specific functions or how does a model help the practising teacher in class- room teaching learning process?

1. **Guidance:** A model of teaching serves a useful purpose of providing in definite terms what the teacher has to do. He has a comprehensive design of instruction with him through which he can achieve the objectives of the course. Teaching becomes a scientific, controlled and goal-directed activity. Thus, a model provides guidance to the teacher as well as to the students to reach the goal of instruction.
2. **Developing curriculum:** A model of teaching helps in the development of curriculum for different classes at different levels of education.
3. **Specification of instructional material:** A model of teaching specifies in detail the different types of instructional materials which are to be used by the teacher to bring desirable changes in the personality of the learners.
4. **Improvement in teaching:** A model helps the teaching-learning process and improves effectiveness of teaching.

SOURCES OF MODELS OF TEACHING

Models of teaching have been grouped on the basis of their sources. There are four important sources from which all the models of teaching have been derived. The sources are described as follows:

1. **The social interaction sources:** The models of this category emphasise the importance of social relationship of the person and his instinctual urge to relate himself with others in the society. This type of model increases democratic processes in the society. All models of this category are based on the assumption that social relation is the vehicle of education.
2. **The information processing sources:** The information processing capability of the learner is another source of models of teaching. Information processing means the way in which people handle stimuli,

organise data, sense problems and solve them. The models of this category develop creativity, and general intellectual ability of the learner. They emphasise the use of specific strategies within academic disciplines.

3. **The personal sources:** The third category of models of teaching shares orientation towards the individual person as the source of educational ideas. The models emphasise the processes by which the individual constructs and organises his reality. Personal and emotional life of the individual and their internal organisation as it affects relationship with his environment, are the sources of this category of models.

4. **Behaviour modification as a source:** B.F.Skinner has developed a new theory of learning which he successfully applied in modifying the behaviour of human beings.

INFORMATION PROCESSING-ORIENTED MODELS

Information processing models of teaching emphasise the ways in which the student processes information. The main objective of the models of this category is to help the students develop the methods of processing information from the environment. The models explain the process of information processing from different approaches. For instance, the inductive teaching model developed by late Hilda Taba emphasises the importance of teaching general problem solving ability to procedures for teaching specific thinking processes. The concept development model emphasises the importance of the development of concepts the Advance Organiser Model by Ausubel has confined only to verbal learning and Developmental Model of Teaching by Jean Piaget is based on the process of intellectual development in children and the adolescents.

All the models of teaching under this category aim to develop concepts and systems of inquiry used by the discipline with the assumption that as a student learns the process and ideas of the discipline, he incorporates them into his own system and behaves differently as a result.

Model	**Major Theorist**	**Goals for which most applicable**
Inductive Thinking Model Inquiry : Training	Hilda Taba Richard Suchman	Designed for development of inductive mental processes and academic reasoning or theory building, but these capacities are useful for personal and social goals as well

Science Inquiry	Joseph J Schwab Curricular Reform Movement (1960)	To teach research system of a discipline, but expected to have effect in other domains. (Sociological methods increase social understanding and social problem solving.)
Concept Attainment	Jerome Bruner	To develop inductive reasoning, but also for concept development and analysis.
Developmental Model	Jean Piaget Irving Sigel Edmund Sullivan	To increase general intellectual development, especially logical reasoning, but can be applied to social and moral development (Kohlberg 1966)
Advance Organizer	David Ausubel	To increase efficiency of information processing capacities to meaningfully absorb and relate bodies of knowledge

Information-processing Models

The members of this family of models share an orientation toward the information-processing capability of students and ways they can improve their ability to master information. These models of teaching influence how students process information from their environment. Methods and theories under this family are designed specially to help students acquire and operate on data. Information processing refers to the ways people handle stimuli from the environment, organize data, sense problems, generate concepts and solutions to problems, and employ verbal and nonverbal symbols. Some Information processing models are concerned with the ability of the learner to solve problems, and thus emphasize productive thinking, others are concerned with general intellectual ability. They emphasise concepts and information derived from academic disciplines. It must be stressed that nearly all models from this family are also concerned with social relationships and the development of an integrated, functioning sel, but the route chosen is through intellectual functioning.

Each model has a distinct point of view about how people think and how to affect the ways they operate on information. Models focusing on information processing have come from several sources.

(1) Studies of thinking: The Philosophers/Greeks have theorised about how the mind works and how inductive and deductive thinking function.

– Studies on individual problem solving.

– Computer simulations of mental processes have been developed.

The description of mental process helps in designing a model of teaching to improve thinking. For ex. the study of how individuals form concepts by a psychologist may assist the educator in improving the processes of concept formation. Many models of teaching are built around mental processes, ranging from systems for teaching general problem solving ability to specific thinking processes, such as Inductive Thinking Model and Inquiry Training Model.

(2) Learning theorists: Ausubel, and Jerome Bruner's work on selection of strategies people use to learn concepts.

(3) The scholarly disciplines.

(4) Developmental studies of human intellect: Developmental model from the work of Jean Piaget's intellectual development of children.

Inductive Model of Teaching

Great research work has been done on the process of human thinking since the earliest days of educational writings. Different methods have been developed to explain and improve the way human beings process information and solve problems.

The inductive model of teaching thinking was developed by late Hilda Taba in her experimental studies conducted in the Centra Costa School. In her model, she provides a teaching strategy to improve the student's ability to handle information. She developed three postulates about thinking process as follows:

1. The first postulate is that thinking can be taught.
2. Thinking is an active transaction between the individual and the data. The interactive process is the classroom learning which is facilitated by the teacher who provides instructional materials on which the learners perform certain cognitive operations and organises facts into concepts and draws certain generalisations to hypothesis, predict and explain unfamiliar phenomena. Mental operations cannot be taught directly without working on instructional materials. The teacher can help the students in the process of internalisation and conceptualisation by dissimulating the students to perform complex mental processes, and after progressively less and less direct support.

3. The third postulate is that the processes of thinking evolve in sequential order and the sequence cannot be reversed.

Therefore, according to Hilda Taba, "This concept of lawful sequences requires teaching strategies that observe these sequences."

Syntax: The model uses three strategies which are interdependent and hierarchical in nature. These strategies should be introduced in classroom teaching at the appropriate time when the learner is curious intellectually for a specific type of learning; the sequence of strategies forms the syntax of the model. The student must go through certain mental operations which are not visible in order to perform the activity.

Social system: The model is based on the assumption that in three strategies the atmosphere in the class is cooperative with a good deal of pupil activity. The teacher is the initiator of phases and thus is the major controller of information. The sequences of the activities are determined in advance so the teacher is in a controlling but cooperative position.

Principles of reactions: Hilda Taba provides in her teaching strategies clear and definite guidelines for teaching and responding within each phase. The teacher must see that cognitive tasks are presented at the appropriate time. Through the process of questions, the teacher should establish cognitive functions. The teacher's main task in the course of the strategies is to monitor the ways in which the students are processing information. The teacher should ascertain the readiness of the learners for new experiences.

Support system: Originally, the model was developed to build teaching strategies in social studies, but the strategies can also be applied in other curricular areas. For the successful implementation of the model, large quantities of raw data which can be organised by students are required. The teacher's main job is to help students to process the data in more complex ways and to increase the general capacity of their system for processing data.

Applicability of the model:

(1) The model may be applied to increase the thinking capacity of children.

(2) The model can be applied in all subjects to increase the productive or creative thinking. The applicability of the model is extremely wide.

Science enquiry: (The art of making inference)

Of the several models that engage students in scientific inquiry, we use the work of BSSC (Biological Sciences Study Committee) led by

Joseph J. Schwab (1965) as the primary example from the beginning, the students is brought into the scientific process and helped to collect and analyse data, check out hypotheses and theories, and reflect on the nature of knowledge construction.

This model is drawn from the BSSC materials where each lesson is an invitation to enquiry.

Goals: School designed this strategy to show students how knowledge arises from the interpretation of data.

And that the interpretation of data or even the search for data proceeds on the basis of concepts and assumptions, that change as our knowledge grows.

- to show that as the principles and concepts change, knowledge changes too,
- to show that though knowledge changes, it changes, for a goal we know better and more than we knew before.
- but the possibility that present knowledge is false. Present knowledge is science based on the best tested facts and concepts we presently possess. It is the most reliable, rational knowledge of which man is capable.

Each invitation to enquiry (or lesson) is a case study illustrating a major concept of the discipline. Each lesson (invitation) "poses example after example of the process itself and engages the participation of the student in the process.

In each case a real life scientific study is described however, omissions, blanks, or curiosity are left uninvestigated, which the student is invited to fill (may be by performing the missing experimentation hypothesising to account for data given) and draw the omitted conclusion.

The model

The essence of the BSSC approach is to teach students to process information using techniques similar to those of research biologists – i.e., by identifying problems and using a particular method to solve the BSSC emphasises content and process.

The Michigan Social Science Curriculum Project, (Ronald Lipptt and Robert Fox) this curriculum illustrates how elementary school children can use scientific proceedings to examine social behaviour. Teach the research techniques of social psychology directly to children using human relation content, including their own behaviour. (Inquiry into own behaviour)

Every subject area has at least one text series that is inquiry– oriented or could be easily adapted to this model. An instructor with a clear understanding of the model will easily discuss instructional material that, with a little rearrangement, might provide suitable areas for investigation. Instructors who are quite knowledgeable in their particular disciplines can probably construct their own materials.

Concept Attainment Model

The Concept Attainment Model of teaching was developed by Jerome S. Bruner, Jacqueline Goodrow and George Austin in 1956. The model emerged out of the study of thinking process in human beings. It is based on the assertion that environment is full of tremendously diverse things and it would have been impossible to adjust in it, if human beings had not been endowed with the capacity to discriminate and to categorise things in groups. This process of classifying things in groups, benefits human beings in three ways. First, it reduces the complexity of the environment, second, it gives the means by which we identify the objects in the world and third, it reduces the necessity of constant learning.

Bruner and associates devoted their major work to the description of things, people and events and placed them into categories.

Syntax — The concept attainment is processed through four phases which are described as follows:

1. In the first phase data are presented to the learner. The data may be of any events or people or any other discernible unit. The learner delineates the units of information in various kinds of attributes, the concept was developed from. The learner is encouraged to drive out the concept or principles or discriminatory concept which is being used on the basis of selection of units.

2. This phase begins by analysing the strategies to attain the concepts by the students. Some learners start with broad constructs and gradually narrow down the field or become more specific in their statement of the concept.

3. In this phase, students analyse the kinds of concepts and their attributes in a variety of materials appropriate to their age and experience. The complexity of developing concepts increases with the age of the

learners. Young children may analyse the simple concepts like feeding bottle, cat, dog and family etc. Older children may examine concepts like social status and other more complex. The main purpose of this phase is to increase the knowledge of the nature of concepts and how they are used.

4. In the last phase, students practice forming concepts, teaching them to others through concept attainment games. This phase is designed to help the students become aware of the concept formation techniques and to sharpen the precision with which he develops and uses concepts.

Social system: In the concept attainment model of teaching, the teacher is the controller of the learning. He presents the data and designates it as belonging or not belonging as an examplar of concept but the atmosphere in the class is cooperative. The teacher proceeds closely in tune with the learner's intellectual development.

Principles of reaction: During the flow of the lesson, the teacher wants to be supportive of the students hypotheses about concepts but to emphasise that they are hypothetical in nature and to create a dialogue in which the major content is a balancing of one persons hypothesis against another's. In the later phases of the model, students analyse their concepts and strategies. He should encourage analysis of the merits of various strategies rather than attempt to seek the one best strategy for all people in all situations.

Support system: Concept attainment lesson requires material which has been arranged so that concepts are embedded in the material, the material can be arranged either so that positive and negative examples are pointed out to the student or so that he may have to find out the concept relevant material himself as when he analyses a political approach. It should be stressed that the student's job in a concept attainment strategy is not to invent new concepts, but attain the ones that have previously been attained by the teacher or teaching agent. Hence, the data sources need to be known before hand.

Applicability of the model

(1) The concept attainment model of teaching is widely used in language teaching. Language learning can be viewed as concept attainment in as much as the society has already devised categories of things and labels for those categories.

(2) Teaching of grammar or the syntactic structure of every language is done through teaching the concept of that language.

(3) The fundamentals of mathematics are taught through concept attainment model.

(4) Concept attainment model of teaching can be used in all disciplines. It can be the basis of extensive man-machine systems in modern teaching learning process.

Development Model of Teaching

Developmental Model of Teaching was developed by Piaget, a Swiss Psychologist, who extensively studied the cognitive development in children for more than fifty years. On the basis of his research studies, he generalised certain principles of intellectual development in children and afterwards, he designed teaching strategy from his researches on development picture to gear the things that are done educationally for the youngster to his state of development at any given moment. The second way uses the developmental pattern to generate teaching strategies that are likely to increase mental development or to accelerate it so that it will occur more rapidly than would be the case if the intervention did not take place.

Syntax: The developmental model of teaching operates in two phases in the classroom instruction. In the first phase, the teacher presents a situation in which the learner is confronted with the illogic of his thinking or a problem which is confusing. The confronting situation must be relatively well-matched to the learner's developmental stage in its substance and form. There should be enough familiarity in the confronting situation to permit assimilation and yet, enough newness to require accommodation.

In the second phase the teacher provides guidance for resolution of the discrepancy, the child faces.

Principles of reaction: The most important aspect of the model is to create conducive environment in the class. The teacher must provide physical and social environment appropriate to the developmental level of the learners. The learners should be free to interact with each other and with the teacher. In order to accelerate cognitive growth, the teacher should properly asses the child's level of thought and learning experiences.

Social system: The social system of the developmental model of teaching can range from highly structured to minimally structured. The role of the teacher is to provide conducive environment. He also guides students for enquiry. He is the initiator. The high structured approach may be more suitable for certain age-levels and to particular problem areas.

Support system: The optimal support system is a rich object and resource environment. The teacher who is well acquitted with the developmental sequence and who can create and tolerate a free social environment that permits the students to work the cognitive problems developed in the confrontations, is an essential part of the model.

Applicability of the model

(1) Model can be applied to cognitive and social development.

(2) It can be used in all subject areas where problem in thinking arise.

(3) It can be used for diagnosis and evaluation as well as for instructional purposes.

(4) It can be employed to ensure that a child can operate smoothly in his environment or to specify activities that will accelerate his cognitive growth.

Advance Organiser Model of Teaching

This model comes under the family of information processing models of teaching; it was designed by David P Ausubel. It is an approach to expository teaching.

Focus: To facilitate meaningful verbal learning and retention.

It includes 2 aspects.

(a) Clarity and stability of learning.

(b) A critical approach of ideas in the cognitive structure.

Syntax: includes 2 phases

(1) Presenting the organiser at a general level

(2) Presentation of material.

These phases must be sequential with more meaningful, specific and original activities.

Social System: Teacher has to present the material in a meaningful sequence. With a highly structured learning situation. He also tries to control the intellectual structure which in turn enables him to discriminate between new material from earlier material.

Support System: Depends upon the relationship between conceptional organiser and rest of the content. Arranging of material must be organised as it relates to organiser. Thus accounts for fact to face teaching.

Application

(1) It can be used to teach any subject area.

(2) Accounts for mastering and solving problems.

(3) Brings a link from material to learner.

(4) Accounts for meaningful assimilation of information/ideas.

Models of teaching vary according to whether they are primarily concerned with the way teaching is or with the way teaching ought to be.

Models theories and paradigms – all these three words are not distinguished, but are used as Synonyms.

Synectics (The Personal Family)

Designed to help people break, set and generate fresh ideas and solutions to problems, synectics has a wide range of applications. It is used to widen perspectives on problems, generate more lucid and creative writing and speaking, and induce creative problem solving. Skillfully used, it has the important side effects of increasing empathy and group cohesion.

Example

1. A study of the Effects of Synectics Model of Teaching Science on creativity, problem and solving ability and empathy, (community feeling fosters interpersonal understanding and a sense of community) in secondary school students.
2. Attitude towards science, interest, self in secondary school students.

Controlled Variables– SES, Gender, Gifted and Non-Gifted students.

Much work was done on test of creativity and to define it (theory) to not on how to develop synectics.

Cambridge synectics group

How individuals overcome specific problems.

Creativity I → Mysterious personal element that cannot be understood.

Creativity I → Or quality that may be tested for and taught to anyone.

Synectics is joining together of different and apparently irrelevant elements.

Recurrent psychological states.

(1) Involvement-Detachment

(2) Deferment

(3) Speculation

(4) Autonomy of object

SOCIAL INTERACTION-ORIENTED MODELS

We have categorised models of teaching on the basis of their sources, for instance, social interaction-oriented, information processing-oriented, person-oriented and behaviour modification-oriented models. Here in this section we will describe group investigation and social inquiry models of teaching the models of this category emphasize the importance of social relations which develop in the process of social interaction among individuals. They may be treated as a goal of education or as educational means. Social interaction-oriented models are an attempt to improve society by improving interpersonal relations through democratic procedures. Philosophically, the models of this category assume that education improves the capacity of the individual to reflect on the ways that he handles information's, on his concepts, and his values. A society of reflective thinkers would be capable of improving itself and preserving the uniqueness of individuals. Democratic process is the creation of interaction among the unique, personal worlds of individuals.

Social Interaction Models

Models	Major theorist	Goals for which most applicable designed
Jurisprudential	Donald Oliver, James P. Shaves	To teach the jurisprudential frame of reference as a way of thinking about and resolving social issues.
Group Investigation.	Herbert Thelen, John Dewey	Development of skills for participation in democratic social process through combined emphasis on interpersonal (group) skills and academic inquiry skills. Aspects of personal development are important outgrowths of this model.
Social Inquiry	Byron Maniales, Benjanin Cox	Social problem solving primarily academic inquiry and logical reasoning.

Laboratory Method Model	NTL (National Training Lab) Bethel, Maine	Development of interpersonal and group skills and through this, personal awareness and flexibility.

Jurisprudential (Inquiry) Model

Donald Oliver and James P. Shaver (1966/74) created the jurisprudential inquiry model to help students to learn to think systematically about contemporary inquiry. It is a high-level model for citizenship education. By giving those tools for analysing and debating social issues, the jurisprudential approach helps students participate forcefully in the redefinition of social values.

Goals and Assumption

This model assumes that a society has people who differ in their views and priorities and in this society the social values legitimately conflict with one another. To resolve the complex and controversial issues, the citizens should talk to one another and successfully negotiate their differences (Within the social order). Citizen can intelligently analyze and take a stance of public issues. Olives and Shaver's image of a skillful citizen is of a competent judge.

(Imagine you are a S.C. Judge. Hearing an important case)

- listen to evidence presented
- analyse legal position taken by both sides
- weigh these position and evidence presented
- asses the meaning and provisions of the law
- Make the best possible decisions

To play this role 3 types of competence are required

(1) Familiarity with values of the country as given in the constitution

(2) Competence to clarify and resolve issues (Definitions, facts identifying values).

(3) Knowledge of contemporary political and public issues.

Syntax – (Analysis and Argumentation)

Phase one: Orientation to the case

- Teacher introduces students to case materials (reading and story, film)
- Teacher reviews facts (analyse who did what and why, controversies)

Phase two: Identifying the issues

- students synthesise facts into a public policy issues.
- students select one policy issue for discussion.
- students identify values and value conflicts.
- students recognise underlying factual and definitional questions.

Phase three

Students articulate a position and state basics of position in terms of social value or consequences of the decision (Ex., State should not legislate how much each district school should spend on each pupil therefore it violates local autonomy)

Phase four: Exploring the stance(s), Patterns of argument

4 patterns of argumentation are:

(1) Ask students to identify the point at which a value is violated.

(2) Clarifying the value conflict through analogies.

(3) Asking students to prove desirable or undesirable consequences of a position.

(4) Asking students to set priorities assertiny priority of one value over another and demonstrate lack from violation of second value.

Teacher/student enacting Socratic rule can use one of the 4 patterns.

Phase five: Refining and qualifying the position

Students state positions and lessons for position and examine a number of similar situations. Students qualify positions.

Phase Six: Testing factual assumptions behind qualified positions

- Identify factual assumptions and determine if they are relevant.
- Determine the predicted consequences and examine their factual validity (will their positions hold under extreme conditions imaginable, i.e., will they actually occur)

Principle of Reaction

Teacher Maintain a vigorous intellectual climate where all views are respected; avoid direct evolution of student's opinion.

See that issues are thoroughly explored.

- Probe the substance of students thinking through questioning relevance, consistency, specify, generality, definitional clarity and continuity.
- **Maintain dialectical style:** Use confrontational dialogue, questioning students, assumptions and using specific instances (analogies) to contradict more general statements.
- Avoid taking a stand.

Social system

Has moderate to high structure, with the teacher initiating and controlling the discussion, however, an atmosphere of openness and intellectual equality prevails.

Support system

Source documents that focus on a problems situation are needed.

Application: For Social Science in high school prepared older students and should be modified for lower high school and middle school levels,. For less verbal students, the argumentation of social issues is threatening at first and discussion can be started in groups at first. Until students become fluent (Competent) in the use of Jurisprudential (Inquiry) model teacher directed activity and direct instruction is needed. Gradually it should lead into student-directed discussion.

Group Investigation Model

The group investigation model of teaching was developed by John Dewey and Herbert,

A. Thelen. They combined their views of democratic social process with the use of scientific or other intellectual strategies to help man create knowledge and better social order. John Dewey in his book *"Democracy and Education"* recommended that entire school be organised as miniature democracy in which students would participate in the development of the social system and would, through this participation, gradually, learn how to apply the scientific method to the perfection of human society.

Herbert, A. Thelen drew the basic principles from John Dewey and developed group investigation model of teaching. His model attempts to combine the teaching strategy– from the dynamics of the democratic process and the process of academic inquiry.

Thelen has emphasized in his model for an experienced-based learning situation conducive to the scientific method and highly transferable to later life situations.

His model emerged from his conception of social image of man. In his book *"Education and The Human Quest"* he wrote about education that it has to come from a conception of a social man, " a man who builds with other men the rules and agreements that constitute social reality." Man is a social by nature. A man cannot harmoniously develop without reference to his fellows.

Social, political, economical and religious norms have been established and modified by human beings and transmitted to next generation in the form of culture. According to him, the mutual negotiation of the social order is the essence of the democratic process.

The classroom is a miniature form of the larger society. It has social order and classroom culture and its students care about the way of life that develops there, that is the standards and expectations that become established. Students learn academic domains of knowledge and ultimately to engage in social problem solving.

Syntax: The group investigation model operates in different phases. The first phase of the model begins when the students confront a problem. The problem may emerge from different sources. It may be a verbal one or can be the provision of an experience. It may be provided by the teacher or it may emerge in class discussion in a natural way. If the students react, the teacher draws their attention to the differences in their reaction. As soon as the students become interested in their differences in reactions the teacher encourages them towards formulation of a problem, moving not to structure their problem for them but to induce them to formulate it for themselves. After formulation, the students attack on it to analyse the required roles and to organise themselves. Next, they act and report their result. Finally, the group evaluates the solution in terms of the original purposes of the group.

Social system: The social system of the model is democratic; the problem is initiated or identified by the teacher as objects to study. The activities of the group are emergent with a least external structure. The teacher and the students have equal status.

Principles of reactions: The teacher works as a counselor. He does not intrude structure. He is vigilant to get the children examine what they are doing in terms of the requirements of inquiry-formulation and solution of a problem, personal meanings and reflections.

Support system: The support system is extensive and responsive to the needs of students. Good library is an essential requisite condition of the model. Students need to establish contact with external agency resource and persons to solve their problems.

Applicability of the model

(1) It is a comprehensive model which may be conveniently used in all subject areas.

(2) It is used in formulation and problem solving aspects of knowledge.

Social Inquiry Model

The social inquiry model of teaching was developed by Byron Masslalas and Benjamin Cox. The term inquiry has very recently emerged in educational writings. It is being used in different contexts conveying the different meanings. For instance, inquiry means a general attitude toward child-centered learning and meaning therebys to develop education around the natural inquiry of the child. The other meaning is to use the modes of inquiry of the academic disciplines as teaching models.

Generally, we mean by the term inquiry to develop students capacity to inquire into and reflect on the social nature of life, particularly, the course of their own lives and the direction of their society in order to solve the social problems. Emphasising the importance of inquiry in education they said, " It is our contention that in view of the prevailing conditions in our culture, the single, most important goal of education should be the reflective examination of values and issued of current import."

According to them, one of the functions of school in the modern society is to actively participate in creative reconstruction of the culture. They explored three essential characteristics of the reflective classroom; the first condition is that the inquiry model cannot operate in any kind of classroom. The inquiry model needs an open climate of discussion in which all students put forward their views on a particular problem. The second characteristic of reflective classroom is the emphasis on hypotheses. The discussion oriented around hypothetical solutions. Knowledge is viewed as hypotheses which are continually tested and retested. The teacher and the students collect data from different sources, analyse, revise their notions and try again. The third characteristic of the reflective class room is the use of facts as evidences. "The classroom is recognized as a form where scientific inquiry is engaged." The validation of facts is given the greatest importance in social inquiry model.

Syntax: The models have six phases which are described as follows:

(1) **Orientation:** The first phase starts by developing general statements of the problem for inquiry. Students are encouraged to locate problems in different areas. The problem should be a genuine felt need of the students.

(2) **Hypothesis:** The second phase pertains to the formulation of hypothesis or hypotheses which can serve as guide for problem solving and can be tested.

(3) **Definition:** Students define the problems and other terms used in the hypotheses. Vague and ambiguous concepts are clarified at this stage.

(4) **Exploration:** Students in this phase examine and explore the hypotheses in terms of their logical validity and internal consistency.

(5) **Evidencing:** Students gather facts from different sources to test the hypotheses.

(6) **Generalisation:** On the basis of the analysis of the data, generalisations or statements about the problem are drawn.

Principles of reaction: From the beginning to the end in the inquiry mode, the role of the teacher is very important. He works as a counselor to inquiry, helps the students clarify their position. He guides the students in improving their method of study and works out their plans.

He helps them clarify language, improve logic, becomes aware of ways of being more object, understanding their assumptions and communicate more effectively with one another. His role is reflective as he helps the students understand themselves and find their own ways. He is focussor and counsellor rather than instructor.

Social system: The social system of the model is slightly structured. The teacher initiates the inquiry and sees that it moves from phases to phases. The students, depending on their inquiry abilities, should take major responsibility for the inquiry itself and even carry it through the phases they are able. The inquiry calls for free and opens discussion among a body of equals.

Support system: The important component of the model is the teacher who believes in the democratic discussion and development of leisurely problem solving approach to life, open-ended library resources, access to expert opinion and other sources outside the school life are the other means for the success of the model. A very rich environment of information is necessary to maintain an honest inquiry and this is particularly difficult to provide because one cannot tell in advances what problems will be identified or just what kind of evidence will be seen as relevant to them.

Applicability of the model

(1) The model teaches students how to be reflective about significant social problems.

(2) The model emphasises that social sciences should be learned in the course of the attempt to develop solutions to significant social problems so that the structure and modes of inquiry of the discipline will be seen as they apply to the area of human concerns.

(3) The model attempts to inculcate a respect for the dignity of all human beings and tolerance in dialogue with differing people.

Laboratory Training

The National Training Laboratory has developed and refined approaches to help people to understand social behaviour, learn more effective social skills, and cope with social change. Laboratory training is also called T-group and Process analysis.

The T-group the heart of the lab training model, confronts participants with an instructured learning situation. Lab training is an educational strategy which is based priority on the experiences generated in the various social encounters by the learners themselves and which aims to influence attitudes and develop competencies towards learning about human interaction. The T-group focuses on individual behaviours as well as on group dynamics.

Assumption

Skills of participating in social groups and organisations can be learned through the process of participation.

T-group

Lab training includes the T-group and also didactic experiences and focused experiences. A T-group comprises of 10-12 persons spending from 80-40 hours together as a face to face group situation. Individuals participate as learners and at the same time help others to understand. The information for learning comes from the immediate group experience, and the experienced behaviour, feelings, perception and reactions of individual group members. The trainer is not an authoritative person but facilitates the development of valid communication.

To begin with the T-group portion people are given the vague task of "constructing a group which will meet the requirements of all its members for growth."

Setting for lab training

A new place: Removes old expectations and norms, thus increasing uncertainty about ones behaviour. Because of the new and unfamiliarity, participants are able to experience fully their behaviours.

T-group experiences emphasise these four areas (learning goals);

(1) **Intrapersonal:** Goal is self-knowledge, gains insight into one's own behaviour by feedback.

(2) **Interpersonal:** Relationships of influence, feedback, leadership trust, formation receiving help control, etc., is developed.

(3) **Group dynamics:** Understand condition that facilitate or inhabit group functioning.

(4) **Self-direction:** Students learn how to learn from their observational skills.

Implicit values of lab training

(1) Spirit of inquiry.

(2) Democratic process

(3) Concern for others.

Lab training comprises of 4 major training activities:

(1) **The T-group itself:** A learning group in which self–observation and diagnosis of the groups, growth and development are the primary mean of training.

(2) **Theory session:** Provide a framework for group experiences. It includes the motion of group goals, norms, cohesiveness, power structure, sociometric structure, role function, group building maintenance roles etc,.

(3) **Focussed exercises:** Have specifically enumerated learning goals

Ex., Role-playing – to enact group role problems.

Tape listening – learning skills.

Instrument – observation skills

– consultation skills

(4) **Experimentation:** With a common real life problem of group shares a work setting or professions.

Application

All the lab training – (1) T-group

(2) Theory session

(3) Focused exercise

It can be used by teachers to help individuals study their own behaviour and their relation with others and to help group of children to work together in more difficult situation by using this model

Conceptual Systems

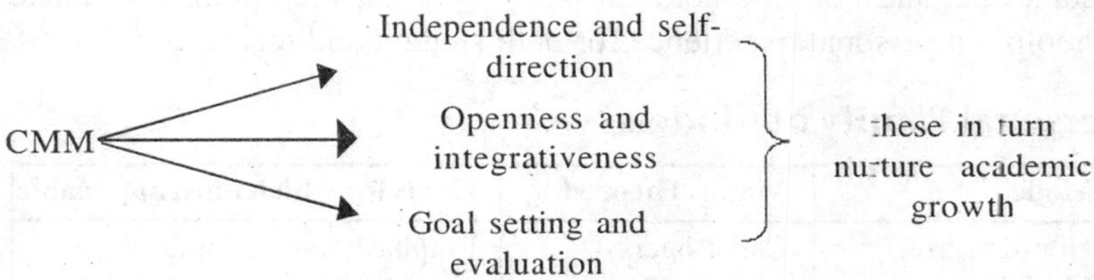

How can we ensure that our teaching methods and models match the development and characteristics of students and help them achieve control over their own growth? Partial answers to these questions lie in the nature of the models themselves. The personal family centers entirely in the student. The social models draw out the values of individuals and involve them in group activity. Information processing models fit the characteristic of the individual. A conceptual system is one such theory, which helps is tailor learning environments to individuals. Conceptual systems theory is a source of ideas for teaching and speaks generally about tailoring models to accommodate individuals (ex., non-directive model; provides no direction. Some people may need more structure than this model provides).

Conceptual systems theory was developed by David Hunt and his associates. The theory describes human development in terms of increasingly complex systems for processing information about people, things and events. Growth is "an interactive function of the person's stage of personality development and the environmental conditions he encounters. Optimal development occurs when the environment facilitates the conceptual work necessary for the person's conceptual growth. As the individual becomes more complex, the environment needs to change with him if growth is to continue at an optimal rate. Hunt helps us to shape teaching strategies to match the learners development, i.e., plan environment to keep people growing conceptually. The closer a teaching strategy is tailored to the less conceptual level, the more learning will take place. Hunt has studied learning characteristics that affect their information processing capacities, such as their motivational orientation, sensory orientation, value orientation (their preferred beliefs) Work on conceptual level (cognitive orientation) is most developed. In conceptual system theory, so this will be concentrated on here.

So first we examine the construct of conceptual level (CL) its implications for the identification of optimal training environment and how to select and modify by teaching according to the theory. Emotional involvement a caring relationship, i.e., a combination of love and discipline.

More traditional views of the school have the teacher as an objective, distant one, and not an emotional one. Therefore the attempts to make schooling a personal experience for both student and teacher.

Personal Family of Models

Model	Major Theorist	Goals for which most applicable
Non-directive Model	Carl Rogers	Emphasis on building the capacity for personal development in terms of self-awareness, understanding, autonomy, and self-concept
(Social Family) Classroom meeting model (Social problem solving)	William Glasser	Development of self-understanding and responsibility to oneself and one's social group.
Awareness Training Model	Fritz Perls	Increasing one's capacity for self awareness and self exploration. Much emphasis on development of interpersonal awareness and understanding, as well as body and sensory awareness.
Synectics Model	William J.J. Gordon	Personal development of Creativity and Creative problem-solving.
Conceptual Systems Model	David Hunt	Designed to increase personal complexity and flexibility.

MODELS OF TEACHING METHODS

Approaches are learning theories which will be applied when delivering subject matter. Methods are a set of teachers' systemic action to reach learning objectives in a limited time frame; it includes procedures based on approaches. Techniques are the manipulation of the method to optimise learning, for example, exercises in class pertaining to a subject matter. A teacher, therefore, is free to construct a teaching method based on an approach. The relationship between approaches, methods and techniques delivers model. Models will explicate teaching methods and strategies, which are in turn based on teaching approaches (Kamaruddin, 1993). Teaching models prescribe tested steps and procedures to effectively generate desired outcomes. The number of emerging models and the ones that have emerged is unacountable. Each emerging new model either explores a new approach or attempts a modification of the conventional ones as to cater to the uniqueness of individuals. Most importantly, any teaching model should optimise learning experiences to the needs of each learner by carefully exploring the learning problems and offering tailored assistance.

How to use models effectively in a classroom

How to use models

In thinking about how to incorporate modeling activities into introductory geosciences courses, there are two important classes of considerations: **technical** and **pedagogical.**

Technical considerations include

- Acquiring the models or ideas in a useable form.
- Identification and use of the proper equipment for physical demonstration models.
- In the case of mathematical models, computers simulations of analogous systems, visualisation models, or statistical models one must learn how to operate and manipulate the modeling environment or software.

These technical considerations are clarified under our discussions related to each specific type of model.

Pedagogical considerations

There are several things to keep in mind when using or creating modeling activities for instruction.

- Keep the activity as interactive as possible. When you find that you're spending a majority of your time lecturing to the students about what to do or how things work, try to think of ways you can get them working through ideas in groups, lab, interactive lectures, etc.
- Including students in the development process and/or providing opportunities for them to experiment with the model or modify it can increase students' understanding of the model and its relationship to the physical world.
- Creating opportunities for students to analyze and comment on the models behavior increases their understanding of the relationships between different inputs and rates.
- Creating opportunities for students to validate the model, i.e., compare model predictions to observations, increases their understanding of its limits.
- Stress that models are not reality and that a model's purpose is to help bridge the gap between observations and the real world. An important reason to use a model is that you can perform experiments with models without harming the system of interest.
- Make sure that students think about the underlying assumptions of a model and the domain of applicability. Try to ask questions that can help check their understanding. For example, simple exponential growth assumes that the per cent growth rate remains fixed and in real world systems it only applies for so long before the system becomes overstressed. Having students identify underlying assumptions of a model and their domain of applicability can help them gain an appreciation of what a model can and cannot do.
- Models can be used to introduce specific content. A model can introduce students to important terms as well as provide an environment to explore relevant processes.
- Models can be used to explore "What-if" scenarios. "What if Atmospheric CO2 doubles?" is a common example for a climate model.

EXERCISES

1. Briefly explain Meaning, Nature and features of Models of teaching.
2. What are the Elements of a Model?
3. Briefly State Characteristics of a Model of Teaching.
4. Mention the Information Processing Family of Models.
5. Mention the Social-interaction Family of Models.

6. Mention the Personal Family of Models.
7. Briefly Explain Concept Attainment Model.
8. Briefly State Laboratory Training Model.
9. How to use Models Effectively in a Classroom?

Chapter 7

Technology in Teaching

Objectives

After reading this unit, you should be able to:

- Classify the Types of Instructional Aids
- Explain Meaning and Nature of Multimedia
- Explain the Procedure for Adopting Multimedia Approach
- State role of Teacher in Multimedia Approach
- Explain the Meaning and Advantages of Computer Assisted Instruction
- Explain how is Internet Learning Beneficial

INTRODUCTION

Classification of Instructional Aids

Non Projected

Chalkboard, Display, Flannel Board, Charts, Maps, Pictures, Posters, Graphs, Objects, Handouts, Cutouts.

Projected

O.H.P, Slide Projector, Film Projector, Slides, Transparencies, Film strips.

Electronic

Radio, Television, Audio, Cassettes, Computers

Non Projected

Chalkboard – Is a simplest type of non projected aid, which is freely available, inexpensive and effective for classroom instruction. It can be made out of wood, round glass, glanoised – known as magnetic boards.

Uses:

1. It is inexpensive, readily available, doesn't need electricity.
2. Used indoors and outdoors, carried anywhere, low maintenance cost, permits a teacher to write important points on the blackboard.
3. Whatever learned on blackboard can be retained for many classes, error can be rubbed out.
4. It can be used by student for illustration and used for combination for other media.

Chalkboard is simplest type of non projected aid readily available for teacher. Though the chalkboard is utilised as encouraging verbalisation and root memories, it is continued to be used by all teacher in education. It is affordable, versatile, commonly available and usable.

Charts: Visual displays arranged on thick sheets. poster papers, newsprint or cardboards. It can be graphic, pictorial or written materials. It is made for different purposes to highlight important concepts, teaching points, diagrams, etc. Charts are supplementary teaching aids for classroom teachers. The classroom teacher must make effective use of charts whenever necessary to make teaching effective.

Charts can be arranged in such a way that they will be able to create one or more visual effects such as:

(a) **Revelation effect:** A chart will be prepared and covered with strip of paper; can be removed whenever necessary. To capture the attention of student and maintain their interest.

(b) **Overlay effect:** A part of chart, which is overlayed by another chart or paper, with help of gums, magnets. To focus upon particular aspect of concepts.

(c) **Flow effect:** Single charts can be displayed one by one, so that they can make a pattern – To show the sequence.

(d) **Magical effect:** To prepare complicated diagrams in advance by using monochromatic harmony. – To explain difficult concepts.

(e) **Dynamical effect:** Very effective to show some monuments on the chart.

A chart is a combination of pictorial, graphic, numerical or verbal material which presents a clear usual summary.

Use of charts:

- It is helpful and handy to the teacher.
- It saves time.
- Flip charts can show a series of visual information.

Boards

Chalkboards.

Merits or uses:

- It needs no electricity, no power dependence and no bill.
- It makes no noise, no motor and no blower
- Use it indoors or outdoors, it comes with you anywhere.
- Gives an all-round visibility.
- No maintenance, no care for a long time.
- Use it on the spot; build up your visuals.
- Use it at your pace.
- Keep written matter on it as long as you like.
- Call a student to write on it.
- Mistakes are rubbed off and corrected instantly.
- Hang your chart on it.
- Place your cutouts on it.
- Use it singly or jointly with other audio visuals.

Display boards

- It communicates information which is colourfully displayed.
- It incites interest and involvement.
- Impart a vitality needed for motivated and purposeful learning.

Graphs: Line graph, bar graph (for numerical representation). Charts can be used either as introductory part, middle or at the end.

Handouts: It is well planned duplicated documents prepared by teacher in order to promote in classroom—Increase interest, motivate students and educate them by being informative.

Different type of handouts

- Summary type
- Completion type
- Note type
- Assignment type
- Laboratory type
- Worksheet
- Question sheet

Summary type: To reinforce keyboard, key statements and principles.

Completion type: It will have information, but will be unlabeled sketch, which you should label, question to be answered, as and when in the classroom.

Note type: Whenever text book is not available, brief notes will be given in the classroom.

Assignment type: Homework, home task, field work, library type.

Worksheet: Problem along with hints will be given for students to complete.

Laboratory sheet: For practical task, table for analysis, question for discussion.

Question sheet: Only objective type of question will be asked and response sheet will be given to enter the responses.

Projected: Aids help the student to retain information for longer time and to make effective use of information, whenever necessary

OHP Advantages

(1) Cheapest and simplest of all aids/ projected visual aids.

(2) It can be used in normal classroom lights and hence, a teacher uses different methods of teaching like discussion method, question-answer method.

(3) OHP projects from large transparencies which are made by hand and machines.

(4) When teacher uses transparencies, she can maintain face to face contact with students while using the transparencies.

(5) Transparencies all prepared in advance with graph, structures, curves, verbal points learning is easier and fast.

(6) Photocopies of transparencies can be circulated to students to activate them.

(7) Transparencies can be made by using different colours.

(8) Transparencies can be used again and again, if it is written with washable ink.

(9) Using transparencies is less stress to teacher.

(10) Less pollutant, relieves teacher from routine task.

(11) It can be pre-arranged.

(12) Used in variety of ways and different colours can be used.

(13) Capture total attention.

(14) Multi–dimensional effect.

(15) High lighting.

(16) Flexibility of use.

(17) Presentation controlled.

Limitations

(1) It can be operated only on electricity, if failure of electricity occurs it cannot be used.

(2) By using overhead projector, it leads to one way communication.

(3) If transparencies are not bold and clear, it will lead to eye strain.

(4) When there is tendencies for teacher to use transparencies too fast, then students may not be able to cope at the speed of the teacher, students may not be able to get the points clearly, and therefore, it leads to confusion and lack of understanding of points.

(5) Colour picture cannot be projected using OHP.

Slides

It is a small transparent visual, usually a transparent picture taken by a still camera on a flame. Slides may either be projected on a screen by a slide projector or be viewed on a slide viewer of 35mm. Standard slide has a film size 24 × 36 mm, in the overall mount dimension. Most slide projectors are suitable for standard slides.

It can bring outside environment inside, create a impact with a use of colour of clarity and sustain the interest of the viewers.

Types of slides

Slides can be prepared as follows:

(1) Slide is made by photographic process.

(2) Computer made slides.

(3) Handmade slides.

(4) Slides may be light slides or flat slides.

(Light slides captures real like object, light slides are events and environment conditions)

(Flat-copy is made by taking pictures of graphic art work and visual drawn on slip of paper, charts or canvas)

Handmade slides: It can be prepared without use of camera and computers.

Simple handmade slides: Are prepared by writing or drawing with fine markers on clear or tinted film.

Disadvantages

(1) Not a very good quality.

(2) It is made in emergency or last minute thought.

(3) We make to add to the existing slides as last minute thought.

Effective use of slides

(1) All slides must be previewed and arranged in proper sequence before the classroom session.

(2) They must be preloaded in a magazine.

(3) Mark the slides.

(4) Slides must be shown frame by frame at slow rate taking care of slow learners.

(5) Should use a long pointer, to point on appropriate side or points.

(6) Teacher must ask questions to students and summarise entire lesson and give some follow-up activities.

(7) Teacher can make use of slides, any number of times in any order.

(8) Slides can be easily revised and updated.

(9) Slides are easy to handle and easy to restore.

(10) Slides are inexpensive to produce.

(11) For effectiveness, slides can be combined with tape narration.

Advantages of slides

(1) A special slides are computer generated. It permits a variety of graphics. Ex: Bar-graph, pie- graph with the help of computer softwares.

(2) It is possible to change the type, font and size of letters at the press of a button.

(3) It is easy to recompose the matter to one's satisfaction.

(4) Easy to change colour of text and background by selecting different components.

(5) It is possible to select thin graphs from readymade graphs software and to add on the desired words upon it.

(6) One can print a slide internally by employing a special camera set-up or externally by photographing the printed flat copy visual.

(7) It is easy to create animation by making a series of slides at short intervals showing an action.

Limitations

(1) Slides are easily damageable.

(2) Sometimes it becomes bulky to store.

Film strips

- It consists of a series of 35 mm pictures, taken on slide strips, film strips are film/strips cut from the film.
- Colour reversed film for slides are loaded into a single frame still camera for making slides and exposed in the same way to result in a series of visuals. If we cut the film and mount individually, we get slides.
- If we don't cut and keep it as a roll, it is a film strip.

Advantages of film strips

(1) Film strips are light weight and easy to transport.

(2) They are not inflammable; hence, there is no danger in carrying anywhere.

(3) Cost of preparation of film strips is not high.

(4) Variety of information may be given by using film strips, information of drawing, map, photographic.

(5) Complete darkness is not necessary when making use of film strips in a classroom.

(6) Even low voltage lamp can serve the purpose of film strips.

(7) The preparation of film strips is easy to be operated by teacher.

(8) With every film strip projector a 2x2 slide attachment is also provided and the same projector is used to project slide also.

(9) Film strips are convenient and flexible to use, when viewed by a group of students.

(10) Film strips are indispensable aid to teachers.

(11) Teachers can monitor pace of the lesson when used.

(12) Teachers can be selective and project that much of material.

(13) By using film strips teacher can also talk.

(14) Film strip projectors are very cheap, readily available and can conveniently make use of film strips by classroom teacher.

(15) Since film strips present the picture in fixed sequence they provide a structure for a subject teacher is teaching.

(16) Film strips provide an economical needs for a classroom teacher.

(17) They are compact and easy to store.

(18) Film strips will usually be numbered therefore it is easy to learners to use it independently.

Limitations of film strips

(1) Don't have simulation commentaries.

(2) Teacher has to do the work of a commentator.

(3) There should be synchronisation of film strips exhibited and teacher's commentary

Electronic Aids

Television

It existed largely because of limitations of radio.

Significance of educational television/advantages

In classroom instruction, television offers variety of opportunity to achieve following clasroom specification.

(1) It is a greater decimal of ideas of knowledge.

(2) Increases realisation of information and usually accompanied by motivation of learning.

(3) Television is capable of carrying different types of symbols, which originate through varied media like speech, music, sound, effects, pictures, diagrams, synematics and gestures. It is accepted as multimedia by itself.

(4) Educational television can add a dimension beyond the range of motion pictures.

(5) It can bring real events which actually happens.

(6) In the case of motion films the event has already been filmed and outcome is not known but in direct telecast the event can be seen as it is occurring in the situations.

(7) Communication by television is effective because it can transmit a wide range of audio-visual materials including picture specimens etc.

(8) Television can bring model of excellence to general viewers and students ex: Speeches by political leaders, poets, teachers, etc.

(9) Television is a mass media that can reach thousands of all over the country. Therefore, television is considered as a great equaliser of educational opportunity.

(10) Television provides sound, sight.

(11) Television saves time, effect of teacher and students.

(12) Acts as feedback technique for teacher.

(13) Provides instructive as well as enjoyable programmes learning process, enhancing curiosity.

(14) Television can overcome barriers of teaching distance, time factor, invisible aspects, class-room size, increase efficiency and effectiveness of teaching-learning process.

(15) Foreign languages can be thought effectively, with help of television programmes.

(16) Science subjects, laboratory, costly equipment, television can be used to telecast those programmes.

(17) It acts as basic report, it compliments other media.

(18) It acts as supplementary enrichments.

(19) In absence of teacher, television programme can be used for children and if there is lack of teacher, if teacher is busy.

Limitations of educational televisions

(1) Costly

(2) Electricity failure.

(3) One-way communication.

(4) Doubts can be clarified

(5) Students miss important points.

(6) Distance between teacher and pupil is limited

(7) No personal contact with teacher.

(8) It will be aimed only at average student, gifted and intelligence are neglected.

(9) Television is small.

(10) Maintenance is expensive

(11) Goals and objectives are to be made clear.

(12) It is only supplementary and complimentary.

(13) Follow-up or feedback is not possible.

(14) Containing all classes students is not possible.

(15) It cannot replace or supplement to teacher. It is only machine, no human touch, it is mechanical.

(16) If there are many divisions of particular class, that are supposed to witness the television programme then it is very difficult to accommodate them all and once at the same time, because such big halls are rarely available in the school.

(17) Television cannot replace the teacher, because it lacks the emotional component.

(18) It can only supplement the classroom teacher.

Classroom utilisation of education television programmes

Whenever a classroom teacher wants to utilise the education television programme, teacher should use following:

(1) Physical environment.

(2) Programme

(1) Physical environment: Education television will be useful if it seen and heard properly by all the students, seeing and hearing will depend upon the following conditions:

(a) A viewing room should be such that there will be enough space to accommodate the audience.

(b) It always should be free from outside noise.

(c) Properly ventilated and at the same time it should be clear and reflection presented is better.

(2) Television set should be kept at a appropriate distance between teacher and learners.

- Protected from extreme moisture and dust.
- Placed on movable table.
- Maintenance should be carried out by expert technicians.
- for maximum visibility, it should be placed at proper height.
- Pupil should look at screen from normal eye light – 30Ú C

Programme utilisation

(1) Depend on willingness of teacher to make full use of educational programme.

(2) Achievement of concrete result through this media.

(3) Adequate time should be allowed for preparation.

(4) Teacher should be clear about statement of objectives.

(5) Teacher exclamatory note of what programme goes to achieve.

(6) Teacher should also suggest learner to supplement and coordinate television.

(7) Programme should be watched by student without interferance.

Audio resources

Radio

- It is inexpensive compared to T.V.
- It provides more localised and need-based programmes.
- Wide coverage.
- Speed and immediacy.
- Ease if access.
- Ease of listening (while eating, walking)
- Thought promotion.
- Ease of programme production.
- All round enrichment.
- Entertain people.
- Secular in nature.

Tape recorder

- Provide motivation.
- Convey information.
- Analyse verbal messages.
- Provide drill and practice or to teach a skill.
- Serve as a study guide.
- Used in convenient time.
- Group listening and discussion.
- For individual self-paced learning.
- Activates listening ability of students.
- Develop power of concentration.
- Active participation and become alert.
- Single tape recorder can reach 100 – together.
- Saves time.

3-D objects and models

- It is inexpensive.
- Convenient to handle.
- Easily available.
- Highly effective.
- Serves as concrete objects.
- Working models can be used to explain easily.
- Students receive correct concept.
- They share direct experience.
- Carried into a classroom.
- Value increases if students handle it.
- Enhance the learning.
- Students are motivated.
- It is re-usable.
- Used to teach pie chart
- Students become active or alert.

MULTIMEDIA

Educational technology is a relatively new field which aims at solving problems of teaching and learning. Hardware and software are two structural components of this technology and multimedia is an important aspect related to them. Education as a system has some objective planned for the process, for the realisation of which a variety of strategies, techniques and aids have been designed and devised by educational technologists. Multimedia approach is one such innovation that is aimed at improving the teaching-learning process.

Nature of Multimedia Approach

- Multimedia approach uses a number of media, devices, and techniques in the teaching-learning process.
- Multimedia approach has come out of researches and experiments in educational technology that have been undertaken in order to improve the process of teaching-learning.
- Multimedia approach aims at providing meaningful learning experiences via mix of media in order to achieve predetermined objectives.
- The choice of the media has to be done carefully so that one does not hamper or reduce the effect of the other, i.e., each media must complement the other.
- The media have to be used sequentially and judiciously. Only necessary ones are to be used. Then it would be possible to make optimum use of them in a most economical manner.

Classification of Media used in Multimedia Approach

The Multimedia approach is an approach that uses a combination of media or strategies. Based on the methods, strategies, modes of instruction or mode of mix the media are classified in the following manner-

Table: Classification of Media in Terms of Methods and Strategies of Teaching

Media

Methods	**Strategies**
(i) Lecture method	(i) Team teaching
(ii) Demonstration method	(ii) Microteaching

(iii) Discussion method

(iv) Lecture-Demonstration method

(v) Heuristic method

(vi) Project method

(vii) Problem solving method

(viii) Inductive-Deductive method

(ix) Laboratory method

(x) Analytic synthetic method

(xi) Question-Answer method

(xii) Assignment method

(iii) Simulated teaching

(iv) Workshops

(v) Group discussions

(vi) Seminars

(vii) Symposia

(viii) Conferences

(ix) Brainstorming

(x) Counseling

(xi) Buzz groups

(xii) Providing practical experiences

Table: Classification of Media on the Basis of Means of Mass Communication

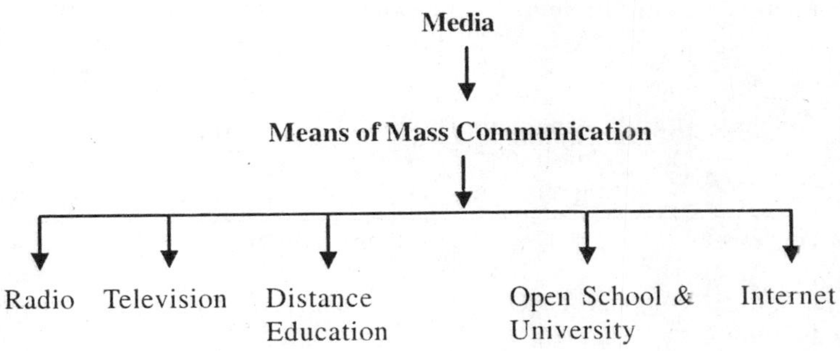

Table: Classification of Media on the Basis of Teaching Aids

Media

↓

Teaching Aids

↓

Graphic	3D Aids	Projective Devices	Mass Communication
(i) Charts	(i) Models	(i) Projectors OHP, LCD, Slides	(i) Radio
(ii) Flash cards	(ii) Specimens	(ii) Filmstrips	(ii) T.V.
(iii) Posters	(iii) Puppets	(iii) Motion picture	(iii) Satellite Communication
(iv) Graphs	(iv) Living and Non-living objects	(iv) Slides	
(v) Diagrams		(v) Transparencies	
(vi) Maps			
(vii) Pictures			

Procedure for Adopting Multimedia Approach

Multimedia approach calls for the use of more than one media in the teaching - learning process. It is imperative that a judicious mix of the several possible media available needs to be done. The following figure. shows the steps to be followed while adopting the Multimedia approach —

- **First Stage:** In this stage the teacher initiates the teaching - learning activities. He sets the ball rolling by delivering a well prepared lesson based on the objectives formulated. He could use a variety of media for his presentation.
- **Second Stage:** In this stage, the teacher demonstrates a specific and specialised unit using a mix of media. The teacher may provide learner with programmed learning materials, cassettes, CD's etc.

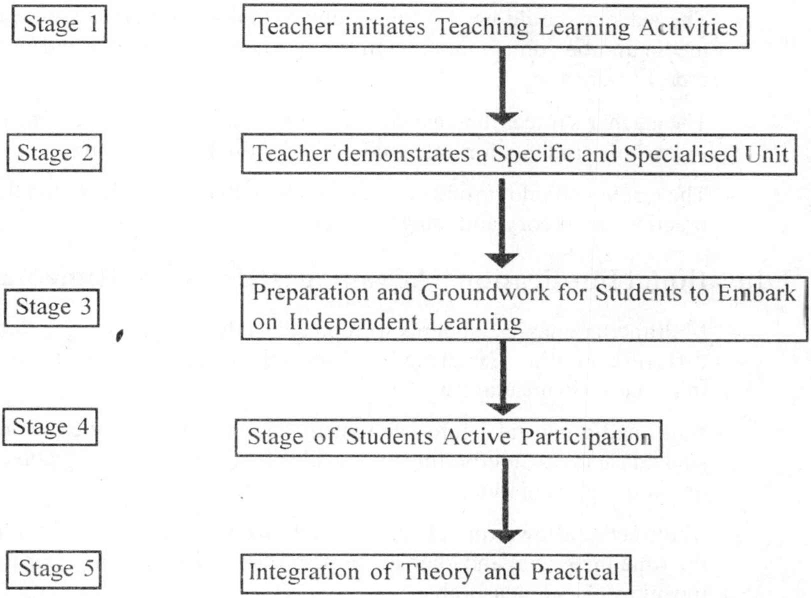

Fig: Procedure for adopting Multimedia Approach

- **Third Stage:** This is a preparatory stage for the learner before he starts independent learning. The student discusses with peer students and teachers his plan of action.
- **Fourth Stage:** In this stage the learner actively participates. He uses a variety of media and materials in his self-study.
- **Fifth Stage:** In this stage the learner integrates theory with practice.
- **Sixth Stage:** In this stage learner finds that teaching learning activities have to be organised on a higher level. He is involved in critical analysis, critical evaluation and exchange of ideas.

Role of Teacher in Multimedia Approach

The teacher has to make a lot of modifications and adjustment if he has to adopt multimedia approach. His role would have a different connotation compared to the traditional role. He would have to make these changes:

- The teacher has to adopt a number of methods and techniques; he cannot be satisfied with the lecture or the chalk-talk method.
- The teacher has to be aware of the different available media and their availability. The teacher should be physically competent to use and demonstrate the use of different media.

- The teacher should be skillful enough to make a judicious choice of media and be competent enough to mix them sequentially and in an orderly manner.
- The teacher's role is that of a facilitator or manager of activities. He has to lead his students for independent, individualised learning.
- The teacher should provide experience such that the students can link practice and theory and integrate them.

Educational Implications/Advantages/Use of Multimedia

- Multimedia enables students to represent information using several different media. Hypermedia links allow students to organise information in meaningful ways.
- Multimedia can take into account different learning styles- Some students learn by interpreting text, while others require more graphical or aural representations.
- Multimedia allows for self-pacing and discovery. Students can take the time they need and choose the path of learning, making learning meaningful and pleasurable.
- Multimedia helps in development of higher order thinking skills. Interactive multimedia encourages students to seek information, apply knowledge and re-attempt tasks (based on feedback given), behaviours that are associated with higher order learning.
- Multimedia provides the students the flexibility of 'anywhere', 'any time' learning.
- Multimedia helps in developing group and interpersonal skills. Better communication between students via e-mail, chat sessions etc., can encourage collaborative learning and enhance student/teacher interactions.
- Multimedia can bridge language barriers since audio is not the only means of communications.
- Multimedia helps students to learn the content in a given discipline. It helps students to think effectively, practice problem solving and decision making.

Thus It has been proved by research that multimedia in schools are effective for students to learn both 'from' and 'with' it. The focus is now on media and technology because of their advantages in terms of repeatability, transportability and equity of access. Multimedia helps students to construct knowledge actively, work in groups and use multi-senses at a time.

That media is power is a well recognised fact. However different media have different potentials. We cannot be rest assured that only one media is suitable for a set of objectives. A judicious mix of media, multimedia helps in removing the limitations of each and cascading the advantages of all.

COMPUTER EDUCATION

Katherine Durack states that "Electronic communications have the marvelous capacity to democratise human communications and to facilitate equal participation regardless of gender, race or disability".

This upholds the need of computer education in a very humanistic manner. Apart from this there are a number of research evidences that speak volumes for the need of computer education. Most of these studies are conducted by USA and UK as they are the countries that extensively use computers. Computerisation is a social process for providing access to and support for computer to be used in teaching, accounting, writing, designing circuits etc., as reported by Dunlop and Kling 1991.

According to Simon- "Computer-based technologies are adopted only because they are efficient economic substitutes for labour or other technologies". Computer-based technologies are simply "power tools" for Information workers or Knowledge workers as drill presses are power-tools for machinists-Strassman (1985).The non-economic dimensions of computerization in particular social settings like small groups, work places, single organisations, comparative multi organisational studies etc.. have also been conducted by Kling and others.

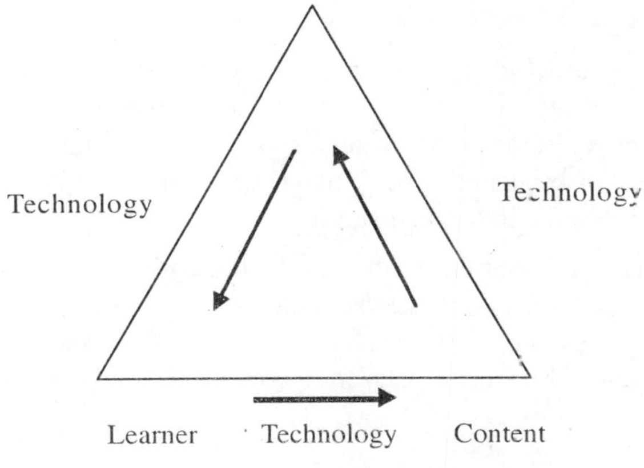

Fig: Need and Process of Computer Education

Computer Assisted Instruction

A computer is going to be utilised as an instructional tool. CAI is considered to be one the best individualised instructions. Computer assisted instruction facilitates learning with the help of computers. CAI has been developed from the principles of programmed instruction.

The basic assumptions of CAI are as follows:-

- CAI can be provided simultaneously even for 4000 students.
- As the learners' performance is going to be recorded automatically in the computer memory, immediate feedback can be provided to the learners by the teachers and also the teachers can use the data in making the best teaching strategy for the learner in future.
- CAI is suitable for all types of teaching and learning activities.

Advantages of CAI

The following are some of the important advantages of CAI–

(a) Self-pacing,

(b) Reteaching and Reinforcing,

(c) Personalised Feedback of Instruction,

(d) Multi–sensory Presentations,

(e) Motivation and Reward and so on.

Instructional Modes of Computer Assisted Instruction

Computer Assisted Instruction (CAI) can be done in many different modes- Some of which are : (i) Tutorial Mode; (ii) Drill and Practice Mode; (iii) Simulation Mode; (iv) Discovery Mode; (v) Gaming Mode.

(i) Tutorial Mode: In this mode, information is presented in small units followed by a question. The pupil's response is analysed and the computer provides appropriate feedback. The programming can be of either linear or branched type. Greater the number of alternative paths, higher would be the individualisation.

(ii) Drill or Practice: In this mode, the computer is programmed to lead the learners series of graded examples on the concepts and principles learnt earlier. All correct responses are reinforced and incorrect responses are diagnosed and corrected. The computer continues the drill until mastery is achieved.

(iii) Simulation Mode: In this mode learner is presented with an artificial, scaled down version of a real life situation. Simulations are designed to avoid risk, conserve time and save money. Examples of simulation are: dissections, nuclear installations, Brownian motion etc.

(iv) Discovery Mode: In this mode the inductive approach to teaching-learning is adopted- The learner is encouraged to proceed through a series of trial and error instances whereby he ultimately solves a problem.

(v) Gaming Mode: This mode is generally recreational but could also be instructional at times. The learner is made to play with computer as his partner. Games of spelling, general knowledge, quiz in Maths and Science are good forms of games where learning also takes place.

ADVANTAGES OF COMPUTER FOR FACILITATING LEARNING

1. The computers guide practice, motivate, involve learners, manage attention, assess proficiency and evaluate progress.
2. It is learner centered, caters to individual needs.
3. It is flexible in terms of time and place (home, office or classroom).
4. Provides opportunity for self-diagnosis and self-study.
5. Adaptive as information can be sequential or random.
6. Computers have total recall and a lot of patience thus dilution does not occur ever after repeated usage.
7. The question of exhaustion does not arise.
8. Specific amount of information is given based on the learner's ability.
9. Learning from experience is possible through simulations.
10. Aids developing of conceptual and abstract skills.
11. Computers also make it possible for varied sensory approach learning and joyful learning through use of colour, shapes, sound, graphic, drawing pads, light pens, joysticks etc.,without the use of stationery to generate these.
12. It can be linked with a variety of electronic media to enhance its educational tools.
13. Cognitive and educational psychologists, classroom teachers, administrators and counsellors can work together to bridge the gap across disciplines and learners.

LIMITATIONS

1. Cost is considered as a drawback.
2. It dehumanizes education.
3. Quality of software is not always assured.
4. With knowledge explosion, information becomes obsolete uncertain becomes very fast thus restricting purchase,
5. Calls for frequent up gradation of knowledge.
6. Requires skilled personnel which makes us think about return on investment.

Thus the classroom teachers are the key to the potential success of the computer being used in education. The greatest challenge for integrating computers into the field of education is countering negative attitudes and tradition. Fear of change, uncertainty, innersystem and concern about technology can be overcome with the teachers support can promote learning with computers by identifying the benefits, developing for motivation utilising advanced organism, designing individual and group learning opportunity, critical evaluation of software and selective utility.

INTERNET LEARNING

Internet is a network of computers. It is the world's largest computer network today. This is nothing but a group of computers linked together. So that they can share information and resources. Actually internet is not a single computer network, but rather a network of networks. Internet has become a popular medium of modern communication

The idea of computer network was conceived in USA in 1969, by the US Defense department. The network was termed ARPANET. Which is the short form of a advanced research project agency networks.

The interest users have access to the internet with the ability to use all the internet tools, including e-mail, file transfer protocol (FTP).

World Wide Web

Internet is the most user-friendly graphical system that offers huge amount of information to the users. A cursory look at Internet would reveal huge sets of pages containing data, information, images, symbols, words, sounds, video clips etc., collected from all over the World. An engineer, Tim Berners Lee, who was working at European Laboratory for Particle Physics, in Geneva, Switzerland, propounded the idea behind the invention of World Wide Web (WWW). This invention was created while working on a method for incorporating footnotes, figures and cross-references into online hypertext documents for the purpose of generating an electronic web of research information.

Tim Berners Lee developed a programming language called Hyper Text Markup Language that allows an author to create hyper links between various types of documents. These hyper text links are the foundation of the World Wide Web. The early web pages contained only textual material, but the emergence of new technologies has provided an opportunity to add pictures and other multimedia elements like sound, voice, images, etc., to the text. Due to advancement in technology. Internet has grown phenomenally over the last few years. At present, there are a great number of Internet Service Providers, browsers/users and many other people who are connected to internet activities– WWW is an interactive graphical system that combines graphics, text, sound, animation etc., into a rich communication media–For the purpose of navigation through various pages, the WWW provides different commands and toolbars. Further, the program Hyper Text Transfer Protocol (HTTP) allows the user to access the universe of information available on internet.

The WWW and HTTP

- Allows one to create "links" from one piece of information to another.
- Can incorporate references to sounds, graphics, movies etc.
- Communicate with other Internet Protocols such as FTP, Gopher and Telnet.

The Web presents information as a series of "documents", often referred to as web pages that are prepared using the Hypertext Markup Language (HTML). Using HTML, the documents author can specially code sections of the document to "point" to other information resources. These specially coded sections are referred to as hypertext

Links. Users viewing a web page can select the hypertext link and retrieve or connect to the information resource that the "link" points to Hypertext links can lead to other documents, sounds, images, databases (like library catalogs), e-mail addresses, etc.

The World Wide Web is non-linear. Non-linear means you do not have to follow a hierarchical path to information resources. Thus

- One can jump from one link (resource) to another.
- One can go directly to a resource if you know the URL, i.e., Its address
- One can even jump to specific parts of a document.

Since the Web is not hierarchical and can handle graphics, it offers a great deal of flexibility in organizing, presenting, and describing the information resources.

Web Page: It is a single unit of information and often called a document, which is available via the World Wide Web. The web pages are created by using HTML. A web page can be longer, than a computer screen, and may require more than one piece of paper when printed. Web pages can be created in different varieties.

Web Site: A collection of related web pages is called a web site.

Web Servers: Web sites are generally housed on web servers.

Web Browsers: A web browser is a piece of software that acts as an interface between the user and the inner workings of the Internet, especially the WWW. The web browsers are also known as Web Clients/Universal Clients. The browser contacts a web server and sends a request for information as designed by the user receives the information and then displays on the user's computer.

Web Master: Is a person or group responsible for designing and maintaining a web site.

Home Page: A web site's primary page is called its Home Page. From his page one can navigate to other pages on the web site.

Uniform Resource Locator (URL): The HTTP uses Internet addresses in a special format called a Uniform Resource Locator (URL). A URL identifies a particular Internet resource. For example, a web page, an image, a text file, a library catalog, a Gopher server etc. URLs represent a standardised addressing scheme for Internet resources. They help the users to locate these resources by indicating exactly where they are. Every resource available via the WWW has a unique URL. The syntax of URL is as follows:

Protocol: //server-name, domain-name, top-level-domain: port/ directory/filename.

The above sentence comprises letters, numbers and punctuations. The hierarchy of this structure moves from left to right. Some examples are:

- http:// stmarysbedcollege.org
- http://luckygreetings.com

Web Searching: The World "Wide Web has emerged as the most reliable and legitimate system of information that can be accessed and retrieved according to certain accepted rules and guidelines. Since large amounts of data and huge information are available .on the web, the specialists have developed three styles of searching. They are:

Surfing: Surfing is an unstructured approach for finding information on the web. Surfing is browsing without tools. One has to make an intelligent guess to arrive at the desired piece of information.

Web Index: The web index is one of the important tools of searching the web that is used to locate information on the www. It is referred to as catalogs or directories. Web index uses hypertext links to present their lists of resources. Most web indexes not only allow users to identify a particular resource of interest; but also actually link them directly to the resource from the index. Due to the vast amount of information available via the web, no single index can contain all possible links to every resource. However, web indexes can include hundreds, ever thousands of resources. Because some web indexes list many resources, they provide a search facility to help user locate resources within the index.

Search Engines / Meta Search Engines: Search engines are powerful interactive data searching tools which help people to locate information on World Wide Web. These engines at databases that contain references to thousands of resource actually search engines provide an interface between us and the underlying database. A place is created by the sear engine to type the request in the form of a word, a phrase, E-Mail and World Wide Web date or any other criterion. The Web search engines use hypertext to link to various resources. By using a search engine and specifying our topic of interest, one can find the right site or information. The web Meta searchers are also tools that provide a single interface to enable the users to explore different search engines, web indexes and databases simultaneously. They do not provide a database but extend services that send a single query to multiple databases.

Accessing and Surfing the net search engines

The Internet is a World Wide network of computer networks. Computer networks are two or more computers linked or connected together by cables or phone links. These computers are linked together to provide seemingly endless amounts of information for research, education, commerce and entertainment purposes. This information is stored on computers called Web servers. Web servers are set up exclusively for internet users to access this information. When you 'surf' the internet you are accessing these millions of computers and receiving the information that they have stored on their web servers.

Internet Addresses (URLs)

Surfing the internet is much possible by the addresses assigned to these linked computers, the web address (also called the uniform resource locator or URLs) allows other computers to view the information as web pages. For example, the Compaq website address is WWW.compaq.com when you access this address the Compaq web site and all associated web pages can be viewed on your internet PC.

Understanding the World Wide Web

The Web is the closest thing to one-size-fits all resource type on the Internet. Through early 1995, the number of servers on the web doubled about every 53 days (According to the Internet society). Any topic or need can be met at least somewhat through information available on the web. This still focus on a Campus and academic information, which you will discover if you try to do search using one of the standard web search tools. But the fastest growing segment of the web is the communal segment business want to use it to tell you about their products and servers and hopefully give you some free and useful information along the way. In the mid 1990s the web offers a little of everything but is not a substitute for the types of information tools you already use, yours telephone and phone books, commercial data bases, encyclopedia and the library in future, the web will replace many of the information tools you now use and some that you haven't even thought of yet.

The Internet is the largest computer system in the world connecting thousands of networks globally. It also enables one to interact with people around the world and download information; no one owns the control of Internet, the different governments, agencies, organisations or companies maintains their own networks.

A few clicks using the mouse transports you to a world that houses voluminous information on unimaginable topics, such as countries, people, news, games, music, arts, organizations and universities to mention a very few. The latest Internet service is the World Wide Web (WWW). A store house of information WWW or W3, with its graphic features is easy to operate, Its collection of documents is called the Web pages and a Web site is a university, government or organization that stores these web pages. Its flexibility lays us the facility to jump form one resource to another. For example- If you are looking for information on pets, it provides you with a list and in addition another, that will supply specific information. We get this via the HTTP (hyper text transfer protocol), Web pages reside on HTTP servers that forward your request for information. Exploration of the web, net surfing or net browsing, to be technically exact, is done with web browse that help to keep the track of the pages you have read. Some of them are the Internet Explorer, Netscape and the Navigator. The web browsers contact the web server and place a request for information, then they receive the same and that is discussed on the server. It always helps to know a few "search engines" when you wander around the net. They are databases that contain extensive reference material, these powerful tools like "Yahoo"," Web crawls" and "Info seek" locate the required information this saves the time and ensures that the user makes optimum use of the time while on line. A part most WWW the Internet is bound by some other major application, UseNet or user network is the largest discussion form in the work consisting of numerous newsgroups, by subscribing to a newsgroup that sends for your internets, you can communicate by writing articles and constructively responding to other articles.

The World Wide Web (www) gopher's internet relay chart (IRC) and E-commerce:

1. A variety of groups and forum are dedicated to special internet areas also.
2. On internet communication can be from person to person computers to computer person to computer.
3. It has emerged as the modern reliable
4. Quick method of communication
5. Information collection also
6. Another special feature of the internet is that no one actually runs the Internet as it's not single network, but a network of networks.

The basic facilities required for an Internet connection required are:

1. Computer
2. A telephone line
3. A modem

4. Software
5. Internet connection

Applications of the internet

1. e-mail
2. News
3. Remote login
4. File transfer

E-mail

The follow of Information through Electronic Media is called E-mail.

The E-mail service is a massage that is encoded as electronic impulses and passed over transmission lines. The message may be memo, letter file, graph, digitised, imaged or combination of any of these.

1. E-mail facility can be considered as a persons post office in home
2. It is a device that enable us to send a message from one computer to another computer
3. It does not need envelop papers or postage stamps and need not wander here and there in search of post office or a post box. The message travels at a speed of light.
4. E-mails eliminates most of the problems and delays of getting a physical document from one person to another
5. The local area network (LAN)— Electronic mail allows users to create send, receive and store message, mail, through this system.
6. E-mail through this system can be send to individual or groups
7. One of the main advantages of E-mail is that no one can open an in box and read delete or add its contents without knowing the inbox owners name and password
8. Another features of e-mail (electronic mail) is the ability to transmit letters, data, files, program, e-files, pictures, photographs, graphs etc
9. To send a message through e-mail a unique address is necessary
10. Electronic mail messages are sent as per the directions of a computer program
11. The internet browsers like Netscape communicator, internet explore mail, send mail, Eudora, explore, can be also be used to send e-mail message

12. Now e-mail has become a very popular communication, medium, and enables. Speedy and reliable transfers of information from one computer to the another.

E-learning

An innovative application of computer in the teaching and learning process is e-learning.

E-learning may be Network-based, Intranet-based or Internet-based, which includes text, video, audio, animation and virtual environments.

E-learning may be stated in the following ways:

- E-learning is learning on Internet time.
- E-learning uses the power of networks, primarily those that rely not only on Internet technologies but also satellite networks, and digital content to enable learning.
- E-learning is the use of network technology to design, deliver, select, administer, and extend Learning.
- E-learning is Internet-enabled learning. Components can include content delivery in multiple formats, management of the learning experience, and a networked community of learners, content developers and experts.
- E-learning provides faster learning at reduced costs, increased Access to learning, and clear accountability for all participants in the Learning process.

The following-are the important features of E-learning:

- E-learning is dynamic.
- E-learning operates in real time.
- E-learning is collaborative.
- E-learning is individual.
- E-learning is comprehensive.
- E-learning is research–oriented
- E-learning is quick learning in short time.

E-learning has definite benefits over traditional classroom training. While the most obvious are the flexibility and the cost savings from not having to travel or spend excess time away from work, there are also others that might not be so obvious.

EXERCISES

1. Briefly Classify the Types of Instructional Aids.
2. Briefly Explain Meaning and Nature of Multimedia.
3. Explain the Procedure for Adopting Multimedia Approach.
4. Briefly State role of Teacher in Multimedia Approach.
5. Explain the meaning and advantages of Computer Assisted Instruction.
6. Explain how is Internet learning beneficial?

Chapter 8

Teaching Effectiveness

Objectives

After reading this unit, you should be able to:

- Explain measurement of teaching effectiveness
- State competency based teacher education
- Explain performance appraisal,
- List out the procedure of performance appraisal

INTRODUCTION

Measuring Teaching Effectiveness

Across the nation, policymakers and education leaders share growing agreement that we must do a better job in measuring effective teaching and identifying effective teachers. And increasingly, there is a belief that measures of effective teaching should contribute to high-stakes decisions like pay for performance and tenure.

But people disagree about what it would take to identify effective teaching consistently and accurately. And many teachers worry that important contributions they make to schools and to the growth and well-being of students will be ignored. Identifying good teaching doesn't and shouldn't have to be a matter of conjecture or opinion. We can build on solid research and create tools that accurately distinguish teaching that leads to student success from teaching that does not. And we can use multiple measures, including student-performance data, classroom observation, feedback from students, and other evidence, to provide well-rounded, fair, and valid input into important decisions.

For most of the high-stakes testing we do in education, we hold the instruments and supporting processes to high technical standards. We must do the same for measures of teacher effectiveness. To implement a robust and defensible system of performance measures, we will have to make sure that such measures are held to higher technical standards than many of today's evaluation tools.

The vast majority of teacher-evaluation tools used today have not been demonstrated to measure what consistently leads to student learning. Most of them represent what particular groups of experts believe is central to good teaching, but very little evidence can be produced to show that these tools identify key components of practice that actually help students learn. Gathering such evidence and validating the tools takes a focused and intensive effort.

Assessments of teacher effectiveness used for high-stake purposes should meet four key technical requirements:

Generalisation: The results of the measure (or multiple measures) must be shown to adequately represent the scope and quality of a teacher's performance. A 15-minute teaching segment is unlikely to convey in depth a teacher's practice, but how much evidence, and what kind, is needed to make a valid judgment?

Evaluation: Scoring rubrics must be well aligned with what is measured, and the scoring itself must be accurate and consistent across time, across evaluators, and across the teachers being measured. This means that we will need to intensify training, calibration, and monitoring among those who observe and evaluate teaching in the classroom.

Extrapolation: We must be able to show that the performance results are a good gauge of our definition of teaching quality. Do high scores for teachers correlate to more or deeper learning for students?

Implication: The use of the performance results must be consistent with the original purpose of the assessment or be shown to be appropriate. An evaluation tool created to check for accomplished teaching, for example, would probably be inappropriate for evaluating the effectiveness of beginning teachers.

The right kind and combination of technically strong measures of teaching effectiveness will not only lead to better judgments about teachers, but also should provide feedback that most teachers don't get today—feedback that could inform their professional growth. In fact, an ideal evaluation system would go hand in hand with teachers' own charting of their course for development and growth, using evaluation and assessment feedback to help in that planning. Imagine an electronic portfolio with not just a teacher's own choice of exemplary work and results, but also data from student assessments and feedback from evaluations, peer coaches, parents and students.

"Many teachers worry that important contributions they make to schools and to the growth and well-being of students will be ignored."

The efforts are moving in the right direction, and with a clear sense of urgency, to expand what we know about the technical qualities of evaluation tools. The Bill & Melinda Gates Foundation is funding a number of projects to identify valid indicators of excellent teaching. These projects are examining the technical quality of several existing assessment instruments, and piloting early versions of new tools, from classroom evaluation tools, to pedagogical content-knowledge tests, to surveys of student perceptions. The data gathered on these tools will be compared with evidence of student outcomes, and combinations of measures will be simulated to determine which "multiple measures" might work best.

These studies are also incorporating innovative ways to gather teaching evidence, including new means of video capture, transfer, storage and scoring. The technical quality of measuring effectiveness, however, does not end with the instruments themselves or the means of collecting evidence. The quality must pervade *how* the measures are implemented, not just what measures are implemented. This means that classroom observation will require a substantial effort to provide adequate training for those who will evaluate, rigorous requirements to show that evaluators are applying scoring criteria consistently, and monitoring or quality-checking of scorers to make sure those judgments stay on track over time and in different classrooms. For teachers who do not teach in grades or subjects covered by state assessments or end-of-course tests, more work is needed in identifying, collecting, and evaluating alternative sources of evidence of student learning. The bottom line is that we must do the work needed to ensure that measures of effectiveness are fair, rigorous, valid, and defensible, and that they result in feedback that teachers can apply to their professional growth. If we want to improve teaching and learning, the right combination of measures, including appropriate use of student-performance data, is a critical part of doing it.

Competency–based Teacher Education (CBTE)

A Strategy for Preparation of Teachers

INTRODUCTION

Competency-based teacher education advocates pressing for consequence competencies as the most important measures of teacher effectiveness. They rely on the ultimate purpose of schools (Pupil learning) as the major rationales for their position. They would hold teachers, accountable for pupil achievement, but would permit a wide range of teacher actions and teaching strategies.

CBTE is a systematic approach for preparing teachers, its concepts are simple and straight forward.

CBTE approach brings about one other major shift from traditional programs. CBTE was developed as a viable response to these two societal forces, with explicit goals and assessment systems, options for participants, prior knowledge of requirements and alternative instructional programs, CBTE offered both individualisation and personalisation. Amid the worldwide actions in CBTE, it must be remembered that, while the concept is sound and fundamental, the implementation is still primitive in terms of its inherent promise. Years of research and development are necessary for adequate testing of the concept.

According to education commission (1964-66): "A sound programme of professional education of teachers is essential for the qualitative improvement of education. Investment in teacher education yield very rich dividends because the financial resources required are small when measures against the resulting improvements in the education of millions".

As stated by Miss W.Walker in "World Trends in Education" (1967): "The function of teacher education is to produce good teachers, The good teacher is one who produces good result in meeting the central persisting needs of life in what ever social context".

Teacher education is needed for kindling the initiative of the teacher, for keeping it alive, for removing the evils of 'hit and miss' process, for according a professional status to the teaching profession and above all for making the optimum use of time and energy of the teacher and the taught.

Meaning of Competency-based Teacher Education (CBTE)

"Competence" is defined as "adequate for the purpose; suitable, sufficient". Or as "legally qualified, admissible", or as "capable". In a sense it refers to adequate preparation to begin a professional career. Competency-based teacher education emphasises a minimum standard; it adds criterion levels, value orientations, and quality to the definition of the movement.

CBTE is based on, and organised around, conceptualisations of effective teacher practice. CBTE programs consider what teachers should know, be able to do and to accomplished requirements based on such outcomes. The term CBTE & PBTE emphasise important elements of the movement – one focusing on objectives, the other on criteria, both are useful for performance and consequence competencies.

History of Competency-based Teacher Education (CBTE)

A growing demand during 1960s for greater relevance in educational practice, a stronger explicit conceptualisations of teacher roles led the United States Office of Education (USOE) in 1967, to request detailed educational specifications that could be used as guides in developing sound teacher –education programs.

Nine sets of specifications were developed during 1968. The following year, eight institutions conducted feasibility studies, which each project had unique educational assumptions upon which its program was based, clearly definable trends permeated all of them. Each program includes objectives, instructional components to meet the objectives, assessment procedures, a design for program management, an opportunity for co-operative interaction, and a systematic approach to comprehensive teacher-education programs. Each relied heavily on feedback from research for improving the program.

Firstly, The accountability that was derived from the commercial and industrial sector of society, with increasing budgets, it was charged that educators should use resources (funds, personnel, buildings) to improve student achievement and that educators should be accountable for such outcomes.

The second force that shaped education was the need for personalisation. Rapid changes in society and technology, combined with an increasingly urban population and more vocational specialisations had led to a depersonalised society.

CBTE was developed as a viable response to these two societal forces, with explicit goals and assessment systems, options for participants, Prior knowledge of requirements and alternative instructional Programs, CBTE offered both individualisation and personalisation.

Around 1970s competency-based teacher education reflected general cultural trends in the United States as well as specific educational goals. The CBTE movement, also referred to as performance-based teacher education (PBTE), Supported by grants from federal, private and state sources, landed as the most effective process to prepare teachers, employed nominally for several years by over 400 institutions.

Five classes of competencies have been defined.

1. Cognitive-based competencies
2. Performance-based competencies
3. Consequence-based competencies
4. Affective-based competencies
5. Exploratory-based competencies

1. Cognitive-based competencies: Define knowledge and intellectual skills and abilities that are expected of the learner (for example, "The prospective teacher can list and illustrate five levels of questions")

2. Performance-based competencies: Define skills and overt actions, the learner demonstrates that he or she can do something rather than simply know something. (For example "The prospective teacher leads a class discussion in which at least 50 per cent of the students participate orally")

3. Consequence-based competencies: The person is required to bring about change in others. Thus, the criterion of success is not what one knows or does, but what one can accomplish. (For example, A teacher's competence is assessed by examining the achievements of pupils)

4. Affective-based competencies: Define expected attitudes and values, and are more difficult to assess than the first three types (For example, the prospective teacher values the contribution of all students in a class discussion)

5. Exploratory-based competencies or (Experience/Expressive objectives): Activities that promise significant learning's are specified. They provide opportunities for students to learn about teaching, but the specific nature of such learning is not defined. Experiences of the learner & the particular set of experience in the activity largely influence the outcomes.

(For example, learner should work 30 hours in a community center. discuss schooling with three parents, or act as a teacher aids for four weeks)

It does not fit well with the four other types in the CBTE classification system.

CBTE programs do not depend on exploratory competencies, but do employ them when precise outcomes have yet to be explicated.

In CBTE, greater emphasis is placed on performance based and consequence-based competencies than on cognitive-based objectives.

Research on CBTE

1. Research basis for this position in psychology through incidental/ intentional learning studies, in experiments in mastery learning by **Ben Jamin Bloom, John Carroll** and their associates, and in the studies of behaviourally stated objectives.

2. Keller's Personalised System of Instruction (PSI)– relied on precise objectives and standards for university science courses. The preponderance of studies tended to support the CBTE hypothesi.

Students who know in advance the specific objectives of instruction achieve more than those unaware of the objectives. CBTE applied this approach to professional training of teachers,

First– Objectives were based on the role requirements of teachers

Second– Performance rather than knowledge alone was required for program completion.

3. Enos at San Diego State University: Enos compared elementary education graduates of a CBTE curriculum track with those of the traditional track, basing his study on the set of objectives the university had certified to the state of California as the basis for their program. He found that CBTE students had significantly greater knowledge about teaching and learning; significantly better verbal interaction with children, significantly greater use of individualised instruction and significantly higher ratings of their performance by children they taught.

4. In dozens of comparisons, made by research, CBTE-trained teachers out-performed graduates of the traditional program.

5. Positive findings favoring CBTE were reported at the University of Nebraska, University of Houston, Weber State University, Oregon College of Education, and University of Toledo.

Such studies generally concluded that CBTE students felt more confident as they completed the program, were evaluated more highly by their supervisors, had a wider repertoire of teaching skills, and believed their preparation program was better than that of other prospective teachers.

The number of documents on CBTE has increased rapidly since the early 1970s.

In 1971, **Allen Schmieder** listed 22 items in his first bibliography on CBTE and 800 items two years later. In 1976, **Cappuzzello** and his associates identified over 6,000 items.

The number of publications on CBTE continued at a steady pace through the early 1980s.

The quality and freshness of their content reflected few new ideas, little research, and no major breakthroughs in problem areas.

The United States federal government supported numerous projects, research, and surveys, encouraging CBTE principles, among them were programs in vocational–technical education, Special education, community education, Teacher corps, Teacher centers, and the elementary teacher education models. In every state, the education agency studied and made recommendations, "Every major professional-education association in the United States was involved during 1970s through task forces, position papers, conference speeches and papers.

Educators from all parts of the world have been involved in CBTE programs. A special one-week training program was sponsored by **UNESCO** in Paris for its chief technical advisors from 60 developing countries.

CBTE programs have been reported in Australia, Brazil, Indonesia, Israel, Japan, Nigeria, Taiwan and the Federal Republic of Germany.

Objectives of CBTE

- To meet at least the minimum standards for each and every competency required in the program.
- To relate achievement to present objectives
- To create a list of competencies in teacher education
- To improve the performance level of teaching-learning process
- To facilitate human relations in all areas of their professional responsibility

- To demonstrate masters of knowledge necessary to implement effective instruction
- To plan and implement instruction effectively to meet the educational needs of their students
- To evaluate their attainment of specified teaching competencies based on student achievement
- To establish learning condition and the learner response.
- To diagnoses the learner's emotional, social, physical & intellectual needs
- To identify or specify instructional goals and objectives based on learner needs
- To design instruction appropriate to goals and objectives.
- To implement instruction that is consistent with plan
- To design and implement evaluation procedures which focus an learner achievement and instructional effectiveness.

Strategies of CBTE

- The Identification of valid competencies based on practices of effective teachers
- Conceptualisations of effective teacher practice
- To determine appropriate teacher-education curriculum and methods that would modify behaviours of trainees.
- Determination of content and organisation of Teacher Education
- To imply adequate assessment procedures to measure the changes in behaviour
- Consider what teachers should know, be able to do and to accomplish
- Providing a systematic approach to handling educational complexity, which will lead to modernising teacher education
- Acquiring master teaching skills and teaching competency objectives.
- The institutions to devote the needed resources to research and refine competencies, programs, assessments and research.

Effectiveness of CBTE

Despite the extensive rhetoric, publications and discussions related to CBTE, almost no basic definitive research was conducted to prove or disprove its effectiveness.

Hundreds of publications recommended ways to design CBTE programs outlined lists of competencies and included instructional units referred to as modules. Few reported research on the CBTE concept, competency validation or program effectiveness; carefully controlled experimental studies were conducted.

The decade of the 1970s, marked the growth spurt of CBTE, four national surveys traced this development. Throughout the decade, the number of institutions operating full-scale CBTE programs increased. By 1980, 80 institutions (13%) reported full-scale CBTE Programs, while 284 institutions were operating small-scale programs.

The per cent of institutions with small-scale programs remained relatively constant 44% in 1975, 49% in 1977, 46% in 1980.

Table: Extensiveness of CBTE Implementation

	Percentage of colleges		
Corresponding Investment (n = 624)	**1973 (n = 783)**	**1977 (n = 570)**	**1980 (n = 686)**
Operating full-scale CBTE program 13	1	8	9
Operating limited CBTE program 45	15	44	49
Exploring or developing CBTE program 14	54	47	26
Not involved 41	29	17	29

A column totals may not total 100 per cent due to overlap in categories of involvement. In its search for ideal preparation for ideal teachers, the findings of one researcher or institution would be shared with others in a growing body of research evidence.

For Example: The research conducted by Enos at San Diego State University shows that CBTE students had significantly greater knowledge about teaching and learning, significantly better verbal interaction with children, significantly greater use of individualised instruction, and significantly higher ratings of their performance by children they taught. In dozens of comparisons, CBTE trained teachers out-performed graduates of the traditional program.

Concern of Critics

Humanistic educators attacked CBTE for its prespecified objectives. Their argument pivoted on whether the learner controlled his own learning or was controlled by some external system. Their view of education as developing free, self-determining, self-renewing, self-actualized persons was antithetical to the basic CBTE conceptualisation. Others charged CBTE with being anti-intellectual with the emphasis in CBTE on performance, they noted that a naïve actor could fulfill requirements without the under girding knowledge base. The specification of competencies was criticised because such lists atomised the teaching process. Teachers do not teach using independent competencies, but in context and using in an integrated fashion a number of skills and knowledge. The value of dissecting general competence into a number of specific and autonomous objectives was questioned. Since each competency was to be measured, the use of a single-variable procedure was considered inadequate. These critics opted for multivariate measures of the total integrated teaching process of a teacher.

Elam (1972,p.21), in his document on CBTE, stated that "The overriding problem before which the others pale to insignificance is that of the adequacy of measurement instruments and procedures". Although hundreds of instruments have been developed and several conferences held on the topic, assessment persists as the major problem in CBTE as in all of teacher education.

No developmental sequence of studies in a comprehensive research program was undertaken; many conclusions were based on the feelings or perceptions of faculty or students. The lack of carefully controlled and constructed research on the effectiveness of CBTE and of specific competencies is a major weakness in development of the movement.

Thus amid the worldwide actions in CBTE, it must be remembered that, while the concept is sound and fundamental, the implementation is still primitive in terms of its inherent promise. Years of research and development are necessary for adequate testing of the concept.The temptation to continue with current programs and not experiment with new approaches must be dissuaded, without the philosophical, pedagogical and psychological analyses that are the essence of CBTE, teacher education will flounder with global goals and complex unanalysed variables only in continual, data-based, thoughtful changes will teacher preparation programs improve. The CBTE approach provides the conceptual frame to make that possible.

Performance Appraisals

Conducting performance appraisals requires a considerable amount of time and energy. It is a tedious process, which can allow personal biases to replace the performance standards.

Negatively viewed appraisals can decrease teacher's morale and employees may gossip and discuss their reviews with others. Performance appraisals can also interfere with the day to day constructive coaching relationship that should exist between supervisor and subordinate.

With the many concerns and numerous "pitfalls" inherent to the performance appraisal process, why should anyone want to conduct performance appraisals? The answer is simple - Employee Morale.

Conducting performance appraisals can be one of the most challenging tasks. However, when done properly, it will be one of your most beneficial tasks. Employees are more motivated and will provide better member service when they feel good about their work environment. One of the primary reasons that employees stay in a job is because of positive recognition they receive from their supervisors. Teachers require honest and constructive feedback about their performances in order to achieve their maximum potential.

Communicating the Performance Appraisal System

Communication is one of the key ingredients in a successful Performance Appraisal System. Numerous methods of communication should be utilised to let employees know that performance standards are important and that they are being observed everyday. Communicating the appraisal process can take place in the employee handbook, job descriptions, in employment agreements, at new hire orientation and during staff meetings.

The old adage of "expect more if you inspect more" holds true with performance appraisals.

In order to communicate the program effectively, some further decisions must be made.

- Will appraisals be conducted semi-annually or annually?
- Will they be tied to salary increase or will raises be a separate activity?
- How do you want to communicate the performance system to the Head and to the employees?
- What is the goal or mission of the Performance Appraisal System (improving member service, professional growth and improvement, etc.)?

The Performance Appraisal System which is communicated only at the time of the review diminishes the effectiveness of the system. It reduces the process to a static system that has no value; instead of becoming a dynamic system that can create a motivating environment where everyone strives to continually improve. This overall communication is the key to a successful Performance Appraisal System. The Head should also receive feedback and updates about the performance appraisal program.

Developing the Appraisal Form

The most effective Performance Appraisal Forms are based upon an objective set of standards. The process of building a Performance Standard System yields valuable information needed to develop training and establish standard operating procedures for the entire operation. Each category of work for a specific position should be ranked based upon various levels of performance.

A Performance Standards System is comprised of:

- Job Analysis – defining units of work and tasks for each position
- Performance Standards – defining what needs to be accomplished for each unit of work
- Job Description – lists all of the above information

Some common elements and categories of appraisal forms should include:

Categories should be related to the job, not subjective in nature – Examples of categories to be avoided include: attitude, initiative, dependability and loyalty.

Categories should be observable and measurable – These might include attendance, quality of work, productivity, appearance, organisation and planning.

Rating scale that ranks the performance of the employee – The best appraisal systems are very specific about each level of performance. Each rating scale, whether it is from poor to excellent or 1-5, should have performance standards to measure each level.

Once completed and properly implemented, a Performance Standards System will improve all aspects of human resource management including. hiring, firing, pay increases, disciplinary procedures, promotions, managerial development and teachers, reward programs.

Conducting the Appraisal

Many Heads are fearful to confront others about job performance. Supervisors need to be coached on the most effective steps to conduct a performance appraisal session. Ten key steps include:

1. Review the employee's personnel file before the appraisal session for any documentation
2. Conduct the review in a quiet area with no distractions
3. Begin the session with small talk for rapport building
4. Reiterate the importance of the appraisal system and why and how it is used
5. Review goals and objectives established from the previous appraisal session
6. Review the self-evaluation form from the employee
7. Review your appraisal of the employee and encourage them to provide feedback
8. Summarise and set improvement goals and objectives with timetables. The employee should sign off on the final appraisal documentation confirming that these items have been discussed and that a plan of action has been made and agreed upon.
9. Thank the employee for participating in the Performance Appraisal System and communicate, again, the goal of the appraisal system
10. Finally, follow up on goals and objectives

Avoiding the "Pitfalls"

There are some specific pitfalls that only affect performance appraisals. All of these are based on a style of delivery of the appraisal as illustrated below:

Communication Approach: This approach leaves the teachers doing all of the listening and reduces the goal setting dialogue. The subjectivity of this style of delivery of the appraisal leaves the teachers questioning the accuracy and validity of the system.

Failure to Listen: This is the teacher's time to talk to the Head and it is important to give the teacher the floor. Failure to listen comes in many forms – interruptions, arguing, becoming defensive/authoritarian, no eye contact, and poor body language. The appraiser should be on the edge of their seat leaning forward, actively listening with eye contact and head nods. The appraiser should show the employee they are listening by asking pertinent follow up questions.

Losing Control: Some employees will bring their emotions into a situation in which their job performance is being reviewed and questioned. If the individual you are speaking to becomes emotional, your best option is to become a passive listener and let them "speak their mind." Once their emotions have subsided, ask if they would like to reschedule the appraisal or continue.

The use of performance appraisals will enable a club's staff to reach peak levels of performance. The appraisal is the best opportunity to give honest feedback to all employees about how they are taking care of the needs of the Institution.

A Performance Appraisal System not only gives a supervisor an opportunity to let employees know how they are performing, it gives the supervisor an opportunity to receive feedback from their employees and set goals for the future. A well-constructed appraisal system creates an opportunity to develop performance – based bonus plans, incentive contests, additional training workshops, form departments, based on appraisal session feedback.

The time and effort dedicated to developing or enhancing a Performance Appraisal System will pay significant dividends through reduced staff turnover, increased employee morale and – most importantly – improved teacher satisfaction.

EXERCISES

1. Briefly explain measurement of teaching effectiveness.
2. Explain competency – based teacher education.
3. What is performance appraisal, briefly state its procedure?

Chapter 9 Tools and Techniques of Teacher Assessment

Objectives

After completing this unit, you should be able to:

- Explain Observation Techniques
- Explain Rating Scales and List out its Types
- State about Inventories
- List out Types of Inventories
- Explain Achievement Test

INTRODUCTION

In orders to make any practical use or interpretation of personality characteristics especially for the particulars individuals, we must have ways of measuring them. We need exhaustive measurements of personality there are variety of different methods to suit these specific purposes which are as follows:

- Observation
- Rating Scales
- Personality Inventories for self-affairs

Observation techniques are used in employing observational methods to study behaviour and interaction in a structured and systematic fashion. They consist of predefined systems for classifying and recording behaviour and interactions as they occur, together with set of rules and criteria for conducting observation and for allocating events to categories. An observation schedule normally will include a time dimension for locating observations in time and will contain variables relating to different aspects of behaviour and interaction, each consisting of a set of categories describing particular behaviours and interactions. The observation schedule is the means by which a teacher operationalised the aspects of the social world that are the focus of the study; it is used to collect systematic and reliable data that can be used in assessment. The categories and definitions used in observation schedules should be explicit and should be capable of being used identically by different observers.

Rating Scales

The rating of one person by others is among the oldest of practices. This type of scale is useful chiefly for learning what impression an individual has made on person with whom he has come in contact in respect to some specified traits or attitudes. The present psychological tools being requirements of the common practice of providing letters and oral recommendations.

While administrating the rating scale, the rating of a particular person are retained from more than one judge, for validity of rating is thereby increased, in as much as subjecting of judgements is decreased.

Characteristics of rating scales:

- The degree of the trait should be defined.
- Reliability depends upon extent of variation of judges rating.
- Overt traits are more reliably rated than covert traits.
- Degree of certainty of rating should be stated.

Types of Rating Scales

The rating scales can be grouped under five categories which are as follows:

(1) Numerical Scales

(2) Graphic Scales

(3) Standard Scales

(4) Rating by Cumulative Points

(5) Forced Choice Rating.

Numerical Scale: In this scale each point as level on the scale carries a specified scale. Each rate checks what he believes to be the correct discretion. The investigator then will convert the check marks into scores.

Example: The idea of making M.Ed., a semester scheme

- Most welcome +3
- Very much welcome +2
- Welcome +1
- Unwelcome -1
- Very much unwelcome -2
- Most unwelcome -3

These scales have tendency, their construction is easy, but these are lightly subjective more than objective.

Graphic Scales: These are very popular and needy used scales have several levels or degrees of the traits are defined and placed at points along a horizontal line.

Example: Quality of teaching done by the science teacher

(a) of Doubtful (b) Not quite (c) Satisfactory

(d) Superior (e) Exceptionally Satisfactory

These scale construction is simple and easy for finer discrimination.

Standard Scales: It is a man to men scale for every quality, five men were to be selected one of quality in the highest order, the four less than that, third is in the middle, the fourth below and fifth in the least.

Example: The error of overestimation and underestimation man and men are not equal.

Rating by Cumulating Points: These can be of the following types. Guess who technique by Hart and may be used to evaluate the children.

Example: Which is the fastest running bird?

Check list method by Harsthan and May, among others and children

Forced Choice Rating: It is a tetrad form of standard scale

Example: Put the correct no in the following:

1. Serious Minded
2. Energetic Minded Favorable (1, 2)
3. Careless Minded
4. Snobbish Minded Unfavorable (3, 4)

To make any of these rating scales accurate it is very essential that these construction should be standardised and record sheet may be prepared.

Uses of Rating Scales

(1) Aid in administration

(2) Encourage the person being rated

(3) Judgements analytical

(4) Useful in research

Inventories

The ratings scales are intended to reveal how other persons perceive the personality of an individual, personality on the other hand are self-rating questionnaires that deal not only with overt behaviour but also with the person's own feeling about himself, other persons and his environment resulting from introspection.

It has been estimated that there are approximately five hundred personality tests and inventories. These would be no point in attempting to describe all of them or even a large number for they have much in common and many of them inferior in conception merit. But all these inventories may be classified into five types.

(1) Assess specified traits like ascendance, conservatism, self-confidence.

Example Bernreuter Personality Inventory:

It is a questionnaire for all grades 9 to 16 and with adults

It consists of 123 items which measures six traits

(a) Reversion (b) Self-sufficiency

(c) Dominancy (d) Covert (e) Lack of self-confidence

- The manner of answering is Yes/No
- Item - do people ever come to you for advice?

(2) Evaluate adjustment to several aspects of the environment like home, school and community.

Example:-California Test of Personality

It has five scales (a) Primary (b) Higher primary (c)Intermediate (d) Secondary (e) Adult

- It consists of 80-94 items
- The manner of answering is in the form of Yes/No.
- The questions are grouped under the categories like:-

(a) Personal Adjustment: Self-reliance, sense of personal worth, nerveless symptoms.

(b) Social Adjustment: Social standard, social skills, school relations.

Item - do you find that a good many people are mean?

Bell Adjustment Inventory

– It is a questionnaire meant for two groups, one kind for adult, other for student.

– It has 140 items which measures four categories

(a) None (b) Health (c) Social (d) Economical adjustment

– The items are to be answered by Yes/No

– Item–are you troubled with shyness?

Classify into clinical groups like paranoiac, psychopathic personality.

Example: Minnesota Multiphase Inventory

– It is meant for 6 years and above

– It consists of 550 items which are pruned on separate cards

– The items are grouped into nine traits like family, general health, attitude and religion Phases etc.

– The items are answered as True/ False/cannot say according to which the cards are sorted into three groups.

– It is mainly used for clinical and diagnostic purpose.

– Administration and scaring requires training and has high predication and validity.

Item - I believe I am being plotted against.

(3) Screen subjects into two or three groups like psychometric disorder vs. normal.

Example:-Cornell Index

– It was denied for the psychiatric and psychosomatic evaluation of large number of persons in a variety of situations

– The questionnaire was standardized for males only.

– It consists of 101 items

– The items fall into the categories which are:

(a) Those differ sharply between people with serious personality disturbances.

- Those concerned with significant bad symptoms
- The items are to be answered by either Yes or No.
- Item–are you laid up to and jittery every moment?

(4) Evaluate interests, values and attitudes like vocational interests, scientific and economic values, attitude towards religion.

Example: Alport - Vernon study of values

- It was designed for the use of college students
- It consists of 45 items the first 30 of which are paired comparison and last 15 multiple choice type resulting into 120 alternatives in all.
- Record each of the choice, represents one of the types of interest or values
- The items are designed to find out the interest in truth, knowledge, social welfare, religion, power and prestige etc.
- The corrected sum of choices of any one kind of items constitutes his score for that type of value.
- Item - believes in religion and goes to temple.

What Is Achievement?

Achievement is generally considered change in cognitive behaviour that we attribute to learning, which can occur both within and outside a planned learning experience, such as a course, class, or training. What students learn can be thought of as existing in one of two related domains. Each domain has a large collection of test items that represent it.

The first domain, which is more familiar to educators, consists of knowledge and skills. We have many examples, including reading, mathematics, and social studies. Generally, States and school districts have content standards that explicitly define each domain. One type of achievement test is intended to be a representative sample from a domain of knowledge and skills. This kind of achievement test is generally created in a selected-response format because of the great efficiency of this format when compared to a constructed-response format. One of the major shortcomings of the latter format is that it does not yield an adequate sample from the intended domain of tasks that represent achievement.

The second domain, which is less familiar to educators, consists of many complex tasks that represent ability. For example, writing is ability. The domain of tasks that represent this ability may include making a report based on some experience; writing a creative story; writing a memorandum, e-mail, or letter; writing an invitation to a social event; and writing a critique, among many others. Many educators and psychologists have suggested that each ability is complex in nature. Each ability is learned slowly and unevenly over a lifetime. Each ability requires the application of knowledge and skills in unique ways to situations that we commonly encounter. The abilities that we learn in school are reading, writing, speaking, listening, mathematical and scientific problem solving, critical thinking, and creative thinking. Most states have adopted content standards that contain learning objectives that describe the kinds of student behaviours that can be tested. The testing format that seems most appropriate for this type of content is performance–based. The scoring of these performance-based tests can be done subjectively, using trained, experienced raters and rating scales, which are referred to as *rubrics*, or the scoring can be done objectively, as we often see in mathematics, where there is likely to be a correct answer or a step-by-step algorithm to apply to reach a correct answer.

Achievement Test

Any test that is designed to measure student learning/teacher assessment in the context of an educational or training program can be called an achievement test. An achievement test comprises one to many test items. Each test item can be scored dichotomously (right or wrong) or with a rating scale, on which degrees of performance are determined by a judge, called a rater. Achievement test items are usually distinguished by the kind of response they generate: selected or constructed. The selected response item is often referred to as multiple choices because the test respondent chooses among the choices offered.

The constructed response item requires that the respondent generate a written or oral response or a response in the form of a product or process. There is considerable variety in selected and constructed response test items. The length of an achievement test varies according to many factors, all of which relate to validity and the intended purpose of the test. One of the most important factors is reliability. Longer tests tend to yield more reliable scores. If an achievement test represents a domain of identifiable knowledge and skills, then it should be a representative sample from this domain. The term *assessment* is often used synonymously with the term *achievement test*. Strictly speaking, the two are not the same. Assessment is a judgment, usually by a teacher, about how well a student has learned and what a student needs to learn. An assessment should be based on valid information, which includes results of achievement tests and other information collected during a semester or school year or in a training program. Thus, an achievement test that is used for an assessment purpose may be given the name *assessment* because the test information is used for an assessment of student learning/teacher assessment.

EXERCISES

1. Briefly Explain about Observation Techniques.
2. Explain Rating Scales and List out its Types.
3. What is Inventories?
4. List out the Types of Inventories.
5. Explain Achievement Test.

Chapter 10 Research Perspectives

Objectives

After reading this unit, you should be able to:

- Explain Research in Teacher Effectiveness
- List out the Research Findings based on Teacher Effectiveness

INTRODUCTION

Research Priorities

In order to maximise the benefits of research investment is very essential. Research meets our current knowledge requirements.

These Research priorities articulate by:

- laying strong educational foundations
- enhancing individual and economic opportunities
- enriching lives and communities
- engaging with others
- improving agility and sustainability

Research priorities with our strategic objectives is intended to stimulate research activity that supports the achievement of these objectives, addresses gaps in our evidence base, and positions to respond to emerging challenges and issues.

Definition of Teaching Effectiveness as an "Act of Faith"

The most accepted criterion for measuring good teaching is the amount of student learning that occurs. There are consistently high correlations between students' ratings of the "amount learnt" in the course and their overall ratings of the teacher and the course. Those who learned more gave their teachers higher ratings (Cohen, 1981; Theall and Franklin, 2001)

This same criterion was also put forth by Thomas Angelo, co-author of *Classroom Assessment Techniques*, when he said **"teaching in the absence of learning is just talking."** A teacher's effectiveness is again about student learning. However, all teachers realie that what a student learns is not always within the teachers' control.

The literature on teaching is crammed full of well researched ways that teachers can present content and skills that will enhance the opportunities for students to learn. It is equally filled with suggestions of what not to do in the classroom. However, **there is no rule book on which teaching methods** match up best to which skills and/or content that is being taught. Students often have little expertise in knowing if the method selected by an individual instructor was the best teaching method or just "a method" or simply the method with which the teacher was most comfortable.

Teachers also have limited control over many of the most important factors that impact students' learning, including students' attitudes, background knowledge of the course content, study and learning skills, time students will spend on their learning, their emotional readiness to learn, and on and on. Since there is clearly a **shared responsibility** between the teacher and the student as to what that student learns, and because many students are able to learn in spite of the teacher, while others fail despite all the best efforts of a skilled practitioner, the definition of "teacher effectiveness" appears to be, as Derek Bok put it, "an act of faith" on the part of students and teachers to do their best.

RESEARCH IN TEACHER EFFECTIVENESS

Recent research reveals that most variation in overall school effectiveness is due to classroom level factors rather than school level factors. For these reasons it is important to try to identify what makes an effective teacher.

Aspects of effective teaching include:

- having a positive attitude
- the development of a pleasant social/psychological climate in the classroom

- having high expectations of what pupils can achieve
- lesson clarity
- effective time management
- strong lesson structuring
- the use of a variety of teaching methods
- using and incorporating pupil ideas
- using appropriate and varied questioning.

However, effective teaching methods are context specific. What is needed for a teacher to be effective can vary depending upon factors such as:

- the type of activity in the lesson
- the subject matter
- the pupils background (such as age, ability, sex, socio-economic status and ethnicity)
- the pupils' personal characteristics (such as personality, learning style, motivation and self-esteem)
- the culture/organisation of the department and school

Research consistently shows that teachers have the greatest potential to influence children's education. "The major research finding is that student achievement is related to teacher competence in teaching," Kemp and Hall (1992, p. 4). Evidence from teacher-effectiveness studies indicates that student engagement in learning is to be valued above curriculum plans and materials. Research on teacher effectiveness has yielded a wealth of understanding about the impact that teacher ability has on student growth.

Highlights of findings from some of the research are as follows:

- Students achieve more when teachers employ systematic teaching procedures (Kemp & Hall, 1992).
- Effective teachers spend more time working with small groups throughout the day (Taylor, Pearson, & Walpole, 1999).
- Greater academic progress occurs when lessons begin with review (Kemp & Hall, 1992).
- Effective teachers use systematic feedback with students about their performance (Kemp & Hall, 1992).
- Teachers who have higher rates of communication with parents are viewed as more effective (Taylor, Pearson, & Walpole, 1999).

- Effective teachers run more orderly classrooms. Achievement has been higher in classrooms where the climate is neither harsh nor overly lavish with praise (Kemp & Hall, 1992).
- Teachers who adjust the difficulty level of material to student ability have higher rates of achievement in their classes (Kemp & Hall, 1992).
- Effective teachers have more students in their classes on task and engaged in learning throughout the day (Taylor, Pearson, & Walpole, 1999). Classrooms in which engaged learning occurs have higher levels of student cooperation, student success and task involvement (Kemp & Hall, 1992).
- Effective teachers clearly articulate rules and include children in discussions about rules and procedures (Kemp & Hall, 1992).
- Effective teachers provide a variety of opportunities for students to apply and use knowledge and skills in different learning situations (Kemp & Hall, 1992).
- Effective teachers are able to pace the amount of information presented to the class, check student progress continually by asking questions of all students, and relate new learning to prior learning (Kemp & Hall, 1992). There is no substitute for a highly skilled teacher.
- Research in other areas indicates that **realizing new learning for all students through professional development** is an important concept. Professional development keeps teachers abreast of current issues in education, helps them implement innovations, and refines their practice.

Research Findings on Student Ratings of Teacher Effectiveness

Research indicates that instructors benefit most from formative evaluation (evaluation meant to improve teaching) when they have helped to shape the questions posed, when they understand the feedback that is provided, and when assistance and resources for making improvements are available (Gaubatz, 2000).

If student ratings are one of several methods used to evaluate a faculty member's teaching (others include peer review, alumni ratings, self-rating, teaching portfolio and informal classroom assessment) the research strongly indicates that few faculty object to their use (Braskamp and Ory, 1994; Centra, 1993a; Doyle, 1983; Seldin, 1999).

Research indicates that **students are the most qualified source to report on the extent to which the learning experience was productive, informative, satisfying or worthwhile.** While opinions on these matters are not direct measures of instructor or course effectiveness, they are legitimate indicators of student satisfaction, and there is substantial research linking student satisfaction to effective teaching (Theall and Franklin, 2001).

A meta-analysis of 41 research studies provides the strongest evidence for the validity of student ratings since these studies investigated the relationship between student ratings and student learning. There are consistently high correlations between students' ratings of the "amount learned" in the course and their overall ratings of the teacher and course (Marsh, 1982; Gaubatz, 2000).

Research on student evaluation of teaching generally concludes that student ratings tend to be reliable, valid, relatively unbiased and useful (Murray, 1994).

1. Evaluations are generally consistent across raters, rating forms, courses and time periods for a given semester
2. They correlate moderately to highly with evaluations made of the same instructor by independent observers
3. They correlate significantly with various objective indicators of student performance, such as performance on standardised exams
4. There are low correlations with extraneous factors such as class size, severity of grading etc. (Murray, 1994).

In short, the research shows that student evaluations of an instructor provide a reliable, valid assessment of that instructor's teaching effectiveness, especially if they reflect the views of many students in several different course offerings (Felder, 2001).

Do Instructor/Instruction Factors Affect Student Ratings?

Students want teachers that have "hardness of head but softness of heart" (Goldsmid, Gruber, and Wilson, 1977). Students want teachers that know what they are talking about but also care about them.

Instructors' Personality Traits: Research has shown that if personality traits affect student ratings it may be caused more by what instructors do in their teaching than who they are as a person (Erdle, Murray, and Rushton, 1985). The personality traits of a teacher are important but have not been seen to invalidate or bias student ratings ((Erdle, Murray, and Rushton, 1985).

Ratings in Elective Courses: Ratings in elective courses are higher than those in required courses. It is suggested by Ory (2001) that **separate norms be established for elective courses, required courses and**

courses that are a mixture of students that are taking a required course with those that are taking the course as an elective. The differences found between these kinds of courses were not overwhelming, but enough variances consistently exist to create separate norms (Costin, Greenough, and Menges 1971; Feldman, 1978; Mc Keachie, 1979 and Marsh 1984).

Level of the Course: The level of the course has a marginal impact on ratings with higher level courses tending to have better course ratings than lower level courses (Aleamoni and Graham, 1974; Bausell and Bausall, 1979; Feldman, 1978; Kulik and McKeachie, 1975).

Innovation/New Course or Revised Courses: New courses usually get **lower than expected ratings** the first time they are taught (Franklin, 2001).

Time of Day: The time of day that a course meets appears to have no influence on ratings (Franklin, 2001).

Class Size: Based on 52 studies of student ratings, Feldman (1978) found **class size** was no serious source of bias, and Centra (1993b) concluded class size had little practical significance.

Different Disciplines: It is suggested evaluators **develop separate norms for different disciplines** as instructors teaching in certain disciplines receive higher student ratings than instructors in other disciplines; however Chiu's 1999 study showed only a 1.19 per cent of rating variance. In descending order the disciplines were **arts and humanities, biological and social sciences, business, computer science, math, engineering, and physical science.** These differences are not large, but they are consistent over many studies.

Gender: There are no signs of any significant relationship between the gender of the instructor and course ratings (Bennett, 1982; Ferber and Huber, 1975; Lombardo and Tocci, 1979; Strathan, Richardson and Cook, 1991). There is, however, some evidence that ratings are slightly higher in classes where the majority of the students are the same gender as the instructor (Feldman, 1993).

Rank, Age and Years of Experience: All of these factors have been shown to have minimal impact on student ratings. **However, first-year instructors** usually receive lower ratings than do experienced instructors (Feldman, 1983) and professors of various rank receive higher ratings than teaching assistants (Brandenburg, Slinde and Batista, 1977; Centra and Creech, 1976).

Race: Race has not been shown to have any biasing impact on ratings (Ory, 2001).

Benefits Student Ratings Can Have for an Institution

Intended Benefits (Ory, 2001)

1. Instructors value the input and make improvements in their teaching
2. Instructors are rewarded for having excellent ratings
3. Instructors with very low ratings are encouraged to seek help
4. Students perceive and use ratings as a way to suggest improvements in teaching
5. Students have more information on which to make their course selections
6. Ratings motivate instructors to improve teaching
7. Students see ratings as a vehicle for change

Unintended consequences ratings can have on an Institution (Ory, 2001)

1. Instructors alter their teaching to get higher ratings including weakening the difficulty of the course or giving higher grades
2. Poor teaching is accepted and overall standards are lowered
3. Campus uses ratings as only measure of effectiveness out of convenience
4. The content of the student rating form may drive what is taught
5. Students reward poor teaching by giving high ratings in exchange for high grades
6. Ratings are used to make discriminations between instructors that are not supported by other data
7. Instructors alter administration of evaluation to get higher ratings
8. The data becomes meaningless because of the lack of use and control

Optimal conditions for students to give instructors feedback (Svinicki, 2001)

1. Students need adequate notice of when they will be asked to give feedback. This will allow for time to think about the questions that will be asked. Ideally students would be informed a day ahead of time that an evaluation will be done so that they can take some time to think about the learning experience and be prepared to give precise and meaningful feedback to the instructor.

2. Students need adequate instruction on how to give the feedback. Students need instruction in how to be precise in their comments and in the definitions of the terms being used in the evaluation. Also students should be informed on how instructors plan to respond to the feedback that the students give.
   - One way to assist students in becoming more precise is to share a sample of student responses from previous evaluations that were helpful in improving the learning experience.
   - Another way is to ask for informal feedback at various times throughout the semester to a few important questions about the learning experience. Share the responses anonymously with the class asking for clarification of responses that were vague or too general and demonstrating how the more precise the students are, the more valuable the feedback becomes.
3. Let students give feedback on a regular basis throughout the semester. Assign a few students in the class to be administrators and summarisers of this feedback process. This can improve the rapport with the students and increase the trust among the students and the instructor leading to students' willingness to be more thoughtful, honest and precise with their feedback on the final evaluation.
4. Students need adequate time to give the feedback. Instructors need to be willing to take class time to get meaningful feedback. Ratings forms should not be given out at the end of the class period as students may tend to hurry so they can leave.

Areas in which students are knowledgeable to share feedback with faculty

These recommendations are based on a synthesis of the many studies that were reviewed and not based on the findings on any one researcher. These are not specific recommendations for what might be used on a ratings form but rather a list of the areas in which students have the experience and knowledge to give feedback.

Students can determine:

1. If the learning objectives set out in the syllabus for the class have been covered by the instructor
2. If they are getting regular and timely feedback from the instructor on their learning progress
3. If the instructor let the class go early and how often has this action occurred
4. If the instructor cancelled class and how often has it occurred

5. If the instructor made it clear as to the time period in which students would receive their assignments and tests back, and kept it
6. If the material that was questioned on the tests was identified by the instructor as being the responsibility of the students to know for the test
7. If the professor was on time for the class each day and how often he/she was late
8. If the professor was available for help outside of class time

   (If he/she was not available the students should indicate how many times this occurred)
9. If the professor kept to the timeframe announced to students that would be used to return students' phone calls or emails
10. If the teacher provided a clear explanation for the grades that were assigned to all work and tests
11. If the instructor spoke clearly and could be easily understood
12. If the professor was willing to answer students' questions during class or provided other opportunities for the questions to be answered
13. If the teacher offered regular encouragement to the students to do well
14. If the teacher sought students' input on issues that directly impacted their learning (discussion guidelines, assessment methods, paper or project topics as examples)
15. If the professor made it clear why (or gave the learning purpose) students were to do the assignments given both in and outside class
16. If the teacher kept the classroom environment positive for learning (didn't allow sleeping, talking, doing other work, phone calls etc.)
17. If the professor knew the names of the students
18. If the textbook or other supplementary material was helpful in their learning of the course material
19. If the professor provided a clear set of learning objectives, or goals, or purpose statements etc., for each class around which students could organise the information they received in the class
20. If the pace of the class was reasonable for them individually
21. If the professor kept to the rules, policies and guidelines outlined in the syllabus

Areas in which students have limited qualifications to give faculty feedback

These questions are based on a synthesis of the research and not based on the findings on any one researcher.

Most students lack the expertise needed to comment on:

1. If the teaching methods used were appropriate for the course
2. If the content covered was appropriate for the course
3. If the content covered was up to date
4. If the motivational methods used were appropriate to the level and content of the course
5. If the assignments were appropriate for aiding student learning
6. If what they learned has real world application
7. If what they learned will help them in future classes
8. If the type of assistance, help or support given to students was appropriate to the learning goals of the class
9. If the difficulty level of the course material was at an appropriate level
10. If the course or the instructor was excellent, average or poor

Suggestions for improving the effectiveness of using a student ratings form

1. Faculty need to continually assure students throughout the semester that the ratings will be used by the faculty for productive change and that there will be no chance of retribution to the students.
2. Faculty need to help educate students in effective ways of giving precise feedback that addresses specific aspects of their learning experience.
3. Faculty need to give students multiple informal opportunities to give feedback throughout the semester, thus practicing their feedback skills. This is also an effective way to improve teaching practice.
4. The university community needs to define key vocabulary words for students that are used in both the formal ratings questionnaires and that they may use in written comments—such words include effectiveness, dependable, organised, reasonable, interesting, excellent, and caring, among others.
5. The university community needs to make certain rating questionnaires are administered in standardised ways including the time of semester and time of the class (beginning of the class).

6. Rating questions need to be limited to those areas in which students have adequate expertise to give meaningful feedback.
7. Those persons interpreting the results of student ratings should be given assistance on how to use the data, its reliability, validity and factors that may impact the results, including the number of students present the day of the rating, whether it's an elective or required course, the type of course and the experience of the faculty member, among other issues.
8. The university needs to assure faculty that ratings data will be collected over several classes before any conclusions about results are made.
9. Those persons interpreting the results need to compare the results with other measures of teaching effectiveness including peer ratings, self-ratings, teaching portfolios, student learning and alumni ratings before any conclusions are drawn about the ratings' information.
10. Faculty need to be assured that ratings are a formative method of evaluation and that assistance to improve their teaching will be made available to them.
11. If a summative use of ratings is to be used it should be the result of multiple courses over several semesters and the intended use of the findings should be made clear to all faculty.

EXERCISES

1. Briefly Explain Research in Teacher Effectiveness.
2. List out the Research Findings Based on Teacher Effectiveness.

BIBLIOGRAPHY

- Alan Januszewski, Educational Technology: The Development of a Concept, Library of Congress Cataloging, 2001.
- Bruce.R.Joyce, Marhsaweil, Emily Calhoun, *Overview-Models of Teaching*, Allyn & Bacon, Inc, 2003,USA.
- Biddle, Bruce.J, and Ellena,- *Contemporary Research on Teacher-Effectiveness*-Hoet Rine- hart and wins Pubs- 353 p,1964, New York.
- Dunkin Michael., J; *The International Encyclopedia of Teaching & Teacher Education*, Pergamon Press, Ist Edition, (P-86-94), 1987, New York.
- Geoff Cumming, Toshio Okamoto, Couis Gomez, Advanced Research in Computer and Communication in Education, IOS Press, 1999, New Zealand.
- Hittlelman, Daniel R – A Model for a Competency Based Teacher Preparation Program- *Teacher Education Forum*-volume 4, Number 12 (P1-14)- 1976, New York.
- Joyce & Well, *Models of Teaching*, 2003, McGraw-Hill.
- Jeaninem Dellolio, Tony Donk: *Models of teaching: Connecting Student Learning with Standards*, 2007, Sage Pub, USA.
- Kumar K.L , Educational Technology, New Age International, 2004, New Delhi.
- Madan Mohan, Ronald. E Hull, Teaching Effectiveness : Its Meaning, Assessment and Improvement.
- Ramnath Sharma, *Advanced Educational Technology*, 2003, Atlantic Pub, New Delhi.
- Ram S : *Modern Teaching Methods*, 1998, Sarup & Sons, New Delhi.
- Sundara Rajan, Chand Tara, *Educational Technology*, 2004, Chand Pub, New Delhi.
- Stephen Petrina, *Advanced Teaching Methods for the Technology Classroom*, 2007, Amazon Pub, USA.
- Shalini Wadhwa, *Modern Methods of Teaching* 2007, Sarup & Sons, New Delhi.
- Sobeih, Nabil Ahmed Amer Competency Based Teacher Education A basic strategy to Educational Improvement Worldwide. *Descriptive Reports* April, 1984, London.

- Tarachand Sharma: *Modern Methods of University and College Teaching*, 2001, Sarup & Sons, New Delhi
- Yin Cheong Cheng, Mafdaleno Moching Mok, Kwok Tung Tsui, 2001: *Teaching Effectiveness and Teacher Development*, Kluwer Academic pub, Hong Kong.
- Zikr-ur Rahman: Modern *Methods of Teaching*, 2005 Sarup & Sons, New Delhi.